# BEHIND CLOSED DOORS

## A Daughter's Story

# Reviews

"A biography/autobiography that I will not soon forget. DeChristopher shares the bitter-sweet story of her mother's and her own life with such candor that I was teary-eyed several times as I read this book."

4 out of 4 stars                    - *OnlineBookClub*

"Daniella DeChristopher is an incredibly brave woman to share her heart wrenching story. I feel she is such a strong woman for everything she endured! I just want to give her a hug for what she went through."

5 stars                    - *HeidiLynnsBook Reviews*

"Obviously, I love the fact that abortion wasn't legal at that time. If not, the author won't be alive today. This clearly defies her achievements so far and the step she took to comfort those going through what she went through. Despite the hardships and abandonment by her own mother, she came out stronger and learned to forgive. Today, she regrets the bad decisions she took and she's happy for the right steps she made. This is a must read, I beckon."

5 stars                    - *Upwrites UK Book Review*

"I think everybody should read this book. It made me inspired optimistic and motivated in my life. It reinsured me that through all the rough times you go through the outcome will always be good in the end."

5 stars                                  *- Jessica Leigh, Goodreads*


"An incredible story seen through the eyes of a child. Nice to know the child in the story became a happy mother and wife. This book gives hope to so many others who do not have a perfect childhood. A story that shatters the idea of the ideal family in the 1950's."

5 stars                                  *- Michele Wrecker, BookBub*


"I loved this book and read it in a day The author writes in a way that makes you feel like you are right there with her as she goes through her journey, I too had a similar childhood and the book made me realize I wasn't alone."

5 stars                                  *- John Rothwell, Amazon*

# Dedication

I dedicate this book to my mother,

who gave up her family

and made personal sacrifices

to allow me to live.

I thank you

from the bottom of my heart.

I love you, I miss you,

and I forgive you.

Your loving daughter,
Daniella

Daniella DeChristopher, LLC

ISBN-13: 978-09995108-0-3

PRINTED IN THE USA

All rights reserved.

Copyright © 2017
#15470774781
This edition published December 2019
Library of Congress Control Number:
TXu- 2-059-262


Melinda Kosztaczky@123RF.com - Tree #10718617

# BEHIND CLOSED DOORS

## A Daughter's Story

Daniella DeChristopher

# Introduction

Millions of people in the world have had to overcome enormous obstacles. They have endured overwhelming pain and suffering for reasons beyond their control. They continue to struggle every day to survive. I haven't walked in their shoes, so I can't imagine what it is like to be them. That's why I don't expect anyone to understand what it was like to be me.

With certainty, there are stories out there far worse than mine. For me, there were times my emotional burden was unbearable. Life seemed hopeless and the sadness I felt was overwhelming.

One day, I realized there was no way I could continue to live the life I had been living. I needed to find a way to create a better life for myself. I decided to stop dwelling on my past and use all my energy to focus on my future.

Many times, I felt discouraged, but I never gave up. It took years of hard work, and despite my unstable childhood, I managed to thrive. I am living proof you can make your dreams come true. My life didn't have a happy beginning; however, I will continue to try to make sure it has a happy ending.

This book is based on actual events. I have chosen to share the embarrassing details of my life in the hope that it will encourage others to put their pasts behind them and try to make a better life for themselves. If exposing the shameful details of mine helps to inspire just one person, then it will have been worth it.

I want to believe people will judge us not by the life we inherited, but by the one we created for ourselves. It should be the *only* one that matters.

# Chapter One

The sound of the cell door slamming shut, hammering against its steel frame, was deafening. I gazed slowly around the room. The walls were unpainted and bare. I could feel the cold of the concrete through my shoes. I saw a bed tucked into the corner. Suddenly, I felt the blood rush to my head and my heart began to pound against my chest. I could hardly swallow. I walked over to the bed, lay down, and curled up in a fetal position. There was a blanket folded at the foot of the bed. I reached down and pulled it up over me. It was thin like a sheet. I was mentally and physically exhausted. I couldn't think. I closed my eyes and drifted in and out of sleep for the next few hours. A woman's shrill voice awakened me.

"It's time to get up. Your food is here. Eat before it gets cold."

The image of the woman was a blur. I could see her place a tray on the shelf under the small barred window. I didn't have an appetite, but I knew I needed to eat. I got up and walked over to pick up the tray. I sat down on the cot and placed the tray on my lap. The smell of the food made me nauseated. I began picking at it, using my fork to move it around my plate. I tried to eat, but I couldn't. I returned the tray to the shelf and began pacing back and forth. I counted my footsteps as I watched an ant disappear into a crack in the floor. Once again, the woman approached my cell.

"You had better get used to the food. You're going to need your strength."

She removed the tray and turned to walk away. I listened to her footsteps as she disappeared down the hall. Suddenly, my life began to flash before me. I thought about William "Billy" Jenson Jr. When I was seven years old, my mom; stepdad, Jason; and I moved into a small two-bedroom starter home in North Florida. Billy and his mom, Jennifer, lived next door to us. Billy was ten years old. Jennifer was a fifth-grade teacher who taught at a nearby school.

Billy's father divorced his mother when Billy was still an infant. A few weeks after the divorce, Billy's dad married his secretary. Growing up, Billy was angry with his father for deserting him and his mom. He felt upset that his dad did not help his mom financially. He never called or visited, and he never bothered to send Billy a birthday card or holiday greeting card. Billy resented the father he never knew. He rarely mentioned him, but when he did, he made it known he had a lot of bad feelings toward him.

His mother didn't make much money as a teacher, and she often had difficulty paying the bills. Somehow, Billy's mom always managed. Despite her struggles, she continued to put money aside for Billy to go to college. She tried hard to be a good mother, making many sacrifices to help Billy have a good future.

Billy took on the role of the man of the house, helping his mother with the household chores. He was protective of her and did everything possible to make her proud of him. It was obvious Billy loved his mother very much. She was kind and generous. I could understand why they were so close. I grew fond of her over the years. She was like a second mother to me.

Billy and I became good friends the day we became neighbors. We played together almost every day and rarely hung out with anyone else in the neighborhood. It was a constant struggle for our parents to separate us. I don't think either of us ever considered that we wouldn't always be together. So when we found out my parents were planning to move, we were heartbroken. On the day of the move, we sat on the steps in front of his home and held each other and cried.

In the beginning, the move didn't affect our friendship. Billy and I worked hard to find time to be together and continued to see each other every chance we could. There were many nights we spent hours talking on the telephone.

One morning, my stepfather, Jason, dropped me off at Billy's house. Billy and I were hanging out watching television. A few hours later, his mother came home and swung open the front door and asked us to step outside. She was glowing with excitement. We got up and headed for the door. There was a beautiful dark-red Mustang convertible parked in the driveway. It had a huge bow on the front and streamers coming from everywhere. Billy's mom knew the Ford Mustang was Billy's favorite car. It was 1965, and Billy had just graduated from high school. She bought it for him for graduation.

Billy's mother handed him the keys. Although he was worried because she had bought such an expensive car for him, he was happier than I had ever seen him. We jumped in, and off we went. He loved driving around and showing off his new car. For months, he picked me up after school. We went for long rides and spent our time together talking about love, marriage, sex, school, and people. There were no secrets between us. He was my best friend.

Not long after Billy graduated from high school, things gradually started to change. He was ambitious and aspired to become a lawyer. He applied to several colleges, and after many months of waiting, Billy finally received a letter of acceptance to a university in Boston. He wanted to become familiar with the area before school started and was anxious to find an apartment. Within a few weeks, he packed and left.

I would often daydream about the two of us together again. I thought about Billy's great smile, blond hair, and crystal-blue eyes. I missed having him in my life. For a while we stayed in touch, but he began calling less often. Eventually, his calls stopped. I tried frantically to keep our connection, but it was out of my control.

Billy finished college many years later and became a lawyer. I often asked his friends how he was doing. They told me he had fallen in love with a girl he met in law school. I hoped it would pass, but it didn't. I'd always thought we would somehow reunite. Then one day, I saw his engagement announcement in the newspaper. Once again, I was heartbroken. Later that year, he married his college sweetheart. She was beautiful; petite, with porcelain-white skin and hazel eyes. His friends told me she came from a wealthy family and had grace and charm. Not long after they married, they bought a five-bedroom house at the beach. The following year, Billy's son was born. They named him Jonathan. They were living the American dream.

When I arrived at the police station, the police officers allowed me one phone call. They hadn't arrested me, but they were holding me for questioning. I didn't understand the process, so I exercised my right to have an attorney present. Although I had not seen or spoken to Billy in years, he was the only person I knew who I thought could help me. I left a message with his office and spent the next few hours in my cell waiting impatiently to hear from him.

I heard someone coming from down the hall. There was a pause and then the jangling of keys. A tall, pale, thin female guard approached my cell.

"Daniella, Mr. William Jenson Jr. telephoned. He will be returning from a business trip today around three p.m. He said he would stop by to see you."

I felt relieved to hear he was coming, but I was nervous about seeing him. What would I say to him? What would he think of me? I was sure I looked a mess. I felt light-headed. I lay down on the bed, but I couldn't lie still. I was a wreck. I got up again and walked back up to the small barred window. The same woman I had seen earlier stepped closer to my cell. I asked her if she had a cigarette.

"What do you smoke?" she asked.

"Menthol, but I will take whatever I can get."

"I'll see what I can find," she replied.

I hadn't smoked in years and couldn't believe I was asking for a cigarette. The thought of smoking again disgusted me, but I thought it might help calm my nerves. I could hear the guard coming around the corner. She walked back up to the window.

"Here you go. It's the best I can do."

She handed me a pack of Camels. I was in no position to request a different brand. I opened them and took one out. I leaned in close to the window and the guard lit it for me, telling me to keep the pack. I thanked her and began smoking my cigarette as I continued pacing back and forth. I finished and walked back over to my bed, where I lay down and closed my eyes. I was fragile and weak. I hadn't eaten much. I felt my skin stretched tightly around my small, delicate frame. I wondered how I would get the energy to get myself through this.

I have often heard people say that everyone has at least one good story in them. I have thought about writing mine hundreds of times. On the surface, I'm sure most people thought I came from the perfect family. We lived in a beautiful house. I don't recall ever needing or wanting anything. We never worried about money. If we did, I never knew about it. No one could ever imagine how imperfect things were. Some of those imperfections were the reason I ended up in here.

It was impossible not to feel sorry for myself. I was twenty-five and sitting in a six-foot-by-eight-foot cell with a barred window. I would never have guessed I would have ended up here. I had been down a very long and complicated road. In an effort to understand why all this had happened to me, I continued to try to sort through the details of my unstable past.

# Chapter Two

My mother, Josie, had a favorite sister named Toni. They were only a year apart in age and had a very close sibling relationship. A short time after my mom died, I called Toni. I told her my mom rarely spoke to me about her life and that I would welcome any information she could give me. Toni said she was happy to share what she knew. She felt it would be best if she started at the beginning. The following is what she told me.

\*\*\*

It began in 1892 in Campania, Italy. Our

parents, Joseph and Adriano DeChristopher, both came from affluent families. In those days, families often used arranged marriages to combine wealth and increase power. By the time Joseph and Adriano were born, both parties' parents had already planned their wedding. When Joseph was sixteen and Adriano was fifteen, they entered into a traditional courting arrangement. The families never allowed Joseph and Adriano to be alone together. After a year of courtship, they became engaged. On the anniversary of their engagement, they married.

Our mother, Adriano, often told stories about her extravagant wedding. She thought it must have been the most beautiful wedding ever held in her country. She said it was everything you would expect from two wealthy Italian families. More than 250 guests were there to celebrate. It was a festive occasion.

Joseph and Adriano had always wanted to travel to the United States. In May 1914, they visited family living in Ohio, bringing their five children with them. They intended to stay for six months, but World War I broke out in August of 1914. Italy's neighboring countries, Austria, Germany, and Russia, were at war. Joseph, feeling it was unsafe to travel, decided it would be best to settle in Ohio.

A year later, Adriano became pregnant. She was pregnant off and on for fourteen years. Big families were the norm in those days. It was common to have what we would think of today as an unimaginable number of children. There were thirteen in total. My sister Josie was the youngest. Our parents raised us with traditional family values.

Joseph and Adriano were loving parents. They taught us to work together by assigning each family member a specific task of responsibility. The girls did the cooking, cleaning, ironing, and sewing. Our father got a job as a supervisor at a brickyard, close to our home, and eventually, our brothers all went to work for him. They were laborers and worked long hours. The work was tiring. Every week they brought their paychecks home. Our strong family union helped us to live a comfortable lifestyle.

Our parents often shared stories of their lives when they were growing up in Italy. They both came from well-established families. They had respect, wealth, and power. Our mother and father often spoke about the family they left behind. They found that living in the states was much different from living in their homeland. However, they created a beautiful life for themselves in Ohio. They were Catholic and Italian and had thirteen children. The family was everything to them. Joseph told his children many times that family was all he needed. He said it made him a very wealthy man. Our parents often talked about the day they would return to Italy to visit relatives, but they never did. They stayed in the family home until they both died in their eighties.

Josie was interested in boys by the time she turned thirteen, and our family knew boys were interested in her. Most girls her age experienced awkward teen stages, but Josie never did. She became a young woman before any of the other girls her age. She was petite and had long brown hair, olive skin, and dark brown eyes. She was stubborn, sassy, and strong-willed. I believe our parents simply didn't have enough energy left to control her.

Josie would wait until she thought everyone was sleeping. She would fluff her pillow, pull up the covers, and climb out of the second-story bedroom window. Some of our sisters would often wake up and beg her not to go, but she did anyway. It was never quite clear where she went. Josie would reappear a short time before anyone awoke and crawl back into bed. A few hours later, she would get up to shower and dress, acting as if nothing had happened. I would often lecture her privately, but it never seemed to affect her. We were very close, but it didn't matter. She never told me where she went.

All of us girls knew Josie had a crush on Nickie Demetrios. We hoped it would pass. Then we found out she was pregnant, and it confirmed our fears. Josie had been sneaking out to see Nickie. Had our father and brothers known, I believe it would have been a sad day for them both.

There were many arguments about Josie's friends. Our parents didn't want her to hang around with them, but she did anyway. She caused the family much worry. With six brothers watching her every move, you'd think it would have been impossible for her to get away with anything, but she was smart and always found a way.

Josie was sixteen when she got pregnant. She lived with her family of fourteen, so the pregnancy was impossible to hide. Never in our family's history had there been a divorce or a child conceived before marriage. The events that followed were heart-wrenching for everyone in our family.

It was 1949 and things were a lot different

back then. We were Catholic and Italian, and abortions were illegal. No one ever spoke about unwed mothers. People considered them spoiled and sent them away. Josie had to drop out of high school in the eleventh grade, because of her pregnancy.

Adriano would sit in her chair for hours and cry. The girls would try to comfort her, but it never seemed to make our mother feel better. Our father was angrier than we had ever seen him. He would blurt things out in Italian. The older children had a better understanding of what he was saying because our parents wanted the younger children to concentrate on learning English. It was just as well we didn't all understand, because our father was furious.

Josie often stayed in her room. She couldn't bear to see the disappointment on our parents' faces. She was sorry for causing the family so much pain. She loved us all, and especially loved our mother. They were very close.

Josie knew it was a matter of time before she would have to name the father of her baby. One night we were in the bedroom, sitting on the bed talking, when our father stormed into the room. We could see the anger on his face. Our mother rushed in behind him.

"Who did this to you?"

He demanded an answer.

Josie held out for as long as she could. She realized she had no choice but to tell the truth. It was heartbreaking to see the devastation on our parents' faces. I watched Josie cup her hands over her face. She began crying as she looked up, pleading with our father.

"Father, please! I beg of you. Please don't send me away."

Our father was getting more upset and spoke with passion.

"Your actions have brought shame to this family. I can no longer allow you to disrespect us in our home. You must tell me now! I will only ask you one more time. Who did this to you?"

I was mindful of Josie's thoughts as I watched her glance at our mother. I knew she could no longer bear to hear her weep and did not want to cause her more heartbreak. Josie knew if she didn't tell our father, it would hurt our mother even more. She looked at our mother one last time and then she looked back at me. I could see the anguish on Josie's face, as she blurted out the name of her baby's daddy.

"It was Nickie, Father. It was Nickie," she cried.

"Nickie Demetrios?" our father shouted at Josie in disbelief. "Please tell me it is not the same Nickie that hangs out on the corner. He is a thug and the black sheep of the Demetrios family. He has caused his parents much pain. He is no good! What are you doing with that bum? Is this the worthless excuse for a man you allowed to impregnate you? Have you no shame?"

Not long afterward, he stormed out of the room. The girls thought for certain our father and brothers would kill Nickie for impregnating Josie.

That afternoon, our father rounded up our brothers, and they headed to Nickie's house for a visit. They were away for several hours and came home just in time for dinner. Dinner was a time the family shared stories of the events of the day. This dinner was awkward for everyone. We hardly spoke a word. The girls were anxious to know what happened at Nickie's house. No one dared to ask.

In February of 1950, there was a private wedding ceremony. By then, Josie was five months pregnant. Josie didn't want to marry Nickie, and

Nickie didn't want to marry her. Unenthusiastically, they married that day. There was no celebration afterward.

Josie wanted to live at home with her family. She begged our father not to make her leave. She tried hard to convince him to let her stay, but he wouldn't listen. Josie was heartbroken. Our father threw her out of the house the night of the wedding. I will never forget his words as he shouted them at Josie: "A woman must live with her husband. You have disgraced this family! You have broken your mother's heart! You must leave now! I never want to see you again! You are no longer my daughter! You and your husband are not welcome in our home!"

He spoke with passion. Josie knew our father would be angry and hurt, but he was more upset than she had ever expected. The girls went with Josie upstairs that night to help her pack. When they finished, they went back downstairs. Our father sent everyone to the cellar except for me, Josie, and our mother. I have often wondered why they allowed me to stay. We could see tears rolling down our mother's face and knew she was in pain. Our mother began pleading with our father: "Please, I beg of you. Do not send our youngest daughter and our first grandbaby away!"

Our father opened the front door. He picked up Josie's luggage and bags of personal items and tossed them outside.

"Go!" he shouted.

He pointed to the road.

"Get out of here. Don't come back!"

As Josie walked out the door, she glanced over her shoulder. She watched our mother fall to her knees.

"Josephina! Josephina!" she cried.

Our mother hadn't called Josie by her full name since the day she was born.

Josie looked down as she picked up her personal belongings. She could see our mother clenching her rosary. Our father began shouting in Italian. It was obvious he was grieving when he slammed the door behind her. I stood there speechless. I couldn't believe what I had just seen. I broke down and cried.

I watched from the window as Josie briskly walked to a car parked at the curb. Nickie was there waiting for her. Josie was crying so hard she couldn't see the pavement in front of her. She stumbled a few times on the way to the car. Nickie opened the back door and tossed her suitcase and bags inside. Josie opened the passenger's side door and got in and they drove away. She didn't look back. She unwillingly went to live with Nickie and his parents.

I thought for certain it would be the last time we would ever see Josie. I quietly went to the cellar, where the others were staying. We all held one another and wept, until we finally went upstairs to bed. The events of the day had devastated our family.

# Chapter Three

Nickie's parents, Sophia and Antonio Demetrios, moved to the states from Greece in the early 1900s. They had four children, Nickie, Seth, Selena, and Simon. Antonio was a smart businessman who built one of the largest department stores in the state. It was a success from the beginning. Seth was the oldest. At the age of twenty-six, he became a partner in the family business. He married a lovely young woman and they had two children. He continued to have a close relationship with Nickie, but Nickie had no connection with anyone else in the family. Simon died of leukemia at the age of fourteen. Selena married a guy she met when she was working as a salesclerk at her family's department store.

My aunt Toni went on to share many of the horrible details of her sister's relationship with Nickie.

One of Seth's friends had introduced Nickie to Josie. Nickie was not very tall, but he was very handsome. He had dark hair and dark eyes and was very muscular. He looked like a street kid and had a reputation for being reckless. Nickie seemed proud of who he had become. It took a lot of courage for Josie to deal with him after they got married, but she had no choice. She had nowhere else to go. Josie said moving in with Nickie and his parents was one of the hardest things she'd ever had to do.

Though abortions were illegal in those days, Josie confessed to me she had often thought about having one. Nickie was constantly reminding her he had people who could take care of it. However, Josie knew if she aborted her child, it would break our mother's heart. She could never do that to Mom. Josie doubted she would ever see her family again, but she refused to destroy any chance she might have. She also struggled with the reality that she was about to become a mother at the age of seventeen. There were still things she wanted to do. She knew her life would change when she became a mother, and that scared Josie most of all.

Immediately after Josie moved in with Nickie and his family, she and Nickie began having terrible fights. They fought constantly, and Nickie repeatedly yelled at Josie at the top of his lungs. She was sure the neighbors could hear him. He was always saying hurtful things to her and called her horrible names. She often felt embarrassed and his words hurt her deeply. Josie's self-esteem was slowly deteriorating. Sophia and Antonio had been kind to her, but Josie worried Nickie's accusations would damage her relationship with them. Antonio would often become enraged. Josie shared stories of many of the arguments she and Nickie had during the time she stayed with the Demetrios family. She said Antonio would always defend her, and not Nickie.

"Lower your voice! I don't want the neighbors to hear you. You are in my home. Don't come here behaving like a crazed animal. What is wrong with you? Josie is your wife! She is having your baby! She is going to be the mother of your child. Show some respect! How can you speak to her that way? How can you call her such awful names?"

When Antonio could no longer tolerate Nickie's lack of respect for Josie, he threw Nickie out of the house.

"You can't continue to yell at her. She cannot stay upset all the time. You are going to make her have a miscarriage. It is unhealthy for her and the baby! I insist you stop treating her this way! This conversation is over. Get out of my house! Now! Do not come back here until you are willing to behave. When you are in our home, you will act civilized."

Antonio felt embarrassed by Nickie's behavior and apologized to Josie for the way Nickie spoke to her.

"I didn't raise my children to behave this way. He has always been a problematic son. He was difficult before he was even born. His mother almost died giving birth to him. We have never liked any of his friends. We have tried to be objective, but they are always in trouble."

After Nikki left, Antonio sat in his chair shaking his head and rocking back and forth. He talked to himself and rambled on endlessly for hours. Josie thought he was having an emotional breakdown.

Nickie's parents were honorable people. They loved her and tried to make her comfortable in their home. They were always trying to cheer her up. Josie knew how hard all of this must have been on them. She would smile, just to make them feel better. Josie often thought of leaving, but she had nowhere to go. She knew someday she would have to move out, and she knew it was going to hurt them.

Nickie and Josie's fights continued to escalate, and each day they were becoming more violent. It didn't matter how many times Antonio demanded they stop. Josie thought it made matters worse. Nickie began pushing and shoving her, and Nickie and Antonio were often shouting at each other. Sophia cried a lot. It was a picture that was all too familiar to Josie. Everyone except Nickie realized how destructive it had become.

There were many nights Josie would sit in a chair next to her bed. She would stare at the wall and try to plan her escape from the hell she had created. She had never loved Nickie and he had never loved her. The pregnancy was just something that happened. She knew he was angry about having to make a commitment to her. Nickie wasn't ready for a child and he felt trapped. They both did.

Josie knew things could not go on the way they were for much longer. She was certain a divorce before her baby was born was out of the question. She would have to wait until she could work and would be able to afford to take care of her baby on her own. She often prayed for the answer to how she would put an end to the madness.

Nickie began to drink excessively and often came home sloppy drunk. There were times he could barely walk through the door and would stumble into the room and fall across the bed. Most nights he was unshaven and unclean and would reek of cheap perfume. The odors were strong and often made Josie sick to her stomach. Time after time, she saw makeup on his clothes, but she didn't care enough to ask where he had been.

There were many nights Josie fell asleep in the chair by the bed. She would get up in the early morning and slip into bed alongside Nickie, praying he wouldn't wake up. She didn't want him to know she had not slept in the bed all night. She was afraid it would be another reason for him to start an argument. Nickie was becoming more violent each day and she didn't want to fight with him when Antonio was not in the room to protect her. She feared Nickie most when he was drunk.

It wasn't a traditional marriage and there wasn't any romance or affection. Josie and Nickie had not had sex since they married. She knew it was only a matter of time before he began demanding it from her, but hoped she was wrong.

Nickie was not husband material. He was aggressive, mean-spirited, and had a nasty temper. He had been destructive his entire life. Nickie enjoyed living his life in the fast lane, and never had a real job and had no intention of ever making an honest living. He was always looking for a new way to scam money. Any time he scammed a dollar, he gambled it away. He loved to gamble and there was no doubt in Josie's mind it was becoming an addiction. She expected he would eventually end up in jail, believing someday the authorities would arrest him for some of the horrible things she knew he had done.

It was hard for Josie to believe his parents were such wonderful people. She wondered how Nickie turned out the way he did. He had so many problems. She wasn't foolish enough to think she could change him into a better man, and she had no interest in trying. She couldn't understand why she had allowed herself to get involved with such a terrible man.

One day Josie and Sophia went to the store. After they got home and put the groceries away, Josie went upstairs. She walked into her room and saw it was in shambles. Nickie was inside pulling out dresser drawers and throwing them on the bed. Everything in the room was out of place. He had emptied the drawers, tossing their clothes and shoes on the floor. Fearing for her safety, she turned to leave, but Nickie grabbed her arms and began shouting at her.

"Where are you going? You're not going anywhere."

He snatched her purse out of her hands.

"How much money do you have?"

Nickie began emptying the contents of Josie's purse onto the bed. He continued to shake it upside down violently and reached in and pulled out her wallet.

She confronted him.

"What is wrong with you? Why are you acting this way?"

"Shut up! I need money!"

"Why do you need money?" she asked.

"I told you to shut up!"

He pushed Josie down on the bed and began removing the money from her wallet and shoving it into his pockets.

"I know you have more. Where is it?" Nickie demanded. He had a very threatening demeanor. "Get it for me, now!" he shouted at her feverishly.

Josie looked toward the door. She was afraid Antonio heard him.

"Please! Keep your voice down. That's all I have. You know I don't have any money. Where would I get money? I have only the few dollars your parents gave me to pay for doctor's visits and pharmacy bills. Where would I get money?"

Josie spoke as softly as she could, hoping to calm him down. Instead, Nickie pushed her back on the bed and grabbed her arms and jumped on top of her. He pulled up her dress, ripped off her panties, unzipped his pants, and forced himself on her. Nickie was hurting her and he knew it, but he didn't care. Josie wanted to scream, but she couldn't. She couldn't let Antonio know what Nickie was doing.

She knew it would be disastrous for everyone. Nickie finished and got up and zipped up his pants. He walked out of the room and slammed the door behind him without saying a word.

Josie lay down on the bed, rubbed her stomach, and cried. She could feel her baby kicking inside of her. It was a reminder of why she tolerated this horrible man. Once again, she began to plan her escape. She eventually closed her eyes and fell asleep. A few hours later, she woke up and went to the bathroom and showered, trying to cleanse herself of the man she had come to despise. She dressed, composed herself, and went downstairs.

Sophia was full of excitement about having a new grandbaby. Josie sat with her that night and talked about decorating the baby's room. Being with Sophia helped her to forget the agony she had endured just a few hours earlier. They planned a picnic for the next day. Neither of them had any intention of inviting Nickie.

Josie noticed that Antonio and Sophia always interacted so kindly with their other children. They spoke often and welcomed their visits. She could see the love they had for one another, and not once did she hear them argue. She never noticed any affection between Nickie and his parents. She wasn't sure they loved him. They were always angry with him. He would get out of bed in the morning and leave before anyone else had awakened. When they did see him, no one bothered to ask him where he was going. His name was rarely mentioned when he wasn't around.

Later that evening Josie went upstairs and sat in the chair by the bed and cried herself to sleep. Nickie never came home that night.

# Chapter Four

*I*n the early morning, Josie headed downstairs. Antonio and Sophia were drinking coffee and eating sweet bread. As they usually did, they greeted Josie with a cheerful hello.

"Good morning, dear. Did you sleep well?" Sophia asked.

Sophia reached into the refrigerator for a bottle of milk and began pouring Josie a glass.

"We set a place for you. We thought you would awaken soon. Would you like me to make you breakfast? Some eggs or French toast?" she asked.

Sophia had such a sweet smile on her face.

Her kindness and generosity always showed through. Josie could tell she enjoyed making the people she loved happy.

"Yes, Mom. That would be nice. French toast sounds great. Are you sure you don't mind?"

Josie sometimes called her Mom. It was her way of showing Sophia love and appreciation for all she was doing for her.

"Of course I don't mind. I wouldn't have mentioned it."

She opened the pantry and began preparing Josie's favorite breakfast as Josie pulled out a chair and sat down. A few minutes later they heard the doorbell ring. Antonio opened the door and saw two police officers standing there. Josie could tell Antonio knew them.

"Carl Simpson and Bob Patterson! What...?"

"May we come in?" asked Bob.

"Certainly, you know you are both always welcome in our home. What can I do to help you today?" asked Antonio.

"Is Nickie here?" asked Carl.

"Why, Carl? What has he done now?"

"Antonio, we have some bad news."

"Get to the point. What has Nickie done now?"

Antonio appeared anxious.

"We have a warrant for his arrest."

"A warrant?"

Josie could see the shock on Antonio's face.

"Nickie has been spending a lot of money he doesn't have. He has been writing thousands of dollars in bad checks. We don't have the exact number, but a lot of people have come forward and pressed charges," explained Carl.

Antonio reached down to grab the arm of the chair. Josie could see his knees buckle. He sat down and rubbed his eyes and placed his hands over his face. Josie could tell Antonio was trying to hold back the tears. When he looked up, Josie could see the worry on his face.

"I have no idea where he is. He comes and goes as he pleases. You know I have never had any control over the boy. He has a mind of his own."

"I'm sorry, Antonio. I know how upsetting this must be. We've been friends for a long time. We wanted to be the ones to tell you," said Carl.

Sophia stood silent as she listened.

"We were fairly sure he wasn't home since we didn't see his car. We didn't want you to be blindsided, because this is going to get messy," said

Bob.

"I appreciate it," said Antonio.

"Antonio, we will be arresting him the minute we find him. We know this is tough. We need for you to let us know if you hear from him," said Carl.

"We certainly will. Please do the same. Let us know if you find Nickie. We would like to know when he is in custody," said Antonio.

"It would be better for him to turn himself in," said Bob.

"If I see him, I'll do what I can," said Antonio.

Carl and Bob moved slowly toward the door.

"Can we do anything, Antonio?" asked Bob.

"No, but thanks for asking."

Antonio opened the door, and Carl and Bob turned and left. Josie, Antonio, and Sophia stood there for a moment, at a loss for words, just looking at one another. They returned to the kitchen table, sat quietly, and finished their breakfast. No one mentioned the picnic again.

Antonio left the kitchen a few minutes later and went upstairs. Josie and Sophia stayed downstairs. They didn't discuss any of it. They talked about decorating the baby's room, then she and Sophia cleaned up the table. They finished tidying up and went into the living room, where they sat on the sofa and drank tea. Later that night Antonio came downstairs and sat in his chair in front of them. He began rocking back and forth.

"Antonio, I think we need to talk about this. We should do something. He is still our son," said Sophia.

"He is no good," said Antonio with disgust. "What should we do? I will not spend the money to buy him out of trouble. I have no interest in doing so. What will he do next, rob a bank? Let his high-roller friends get him out of this one."

That was the end of the discussion. They sat around talking about other things for hours. As they were about to go to bed, the telephone rang. Officer Simpson called to let Antonio know they had arrested Nickie. Antonio didn't give any of the details. He told Josie and Sophia to go upstairs to bed.

Josie suspected Antonio stayed downstairs that night and slept in his rocking chair. She thought he was waiting by the telephone for Nickie to call and ask for help, but he never did.

Josie went downstairs the next morning and found Sophia and Antonio sitting at the table drinking coffee. Antonio was talking on the telephone to the police.

"I'll be down there shortly, I want to have a conversation with the boy so I can get to the bottom of this."

Sophia made breakfast. When they finished eating, Antonio left for the police station. He returned a few hours later, and Sophia asked how things went.

Antonio said Nickie had left by the time he'd gotten there. One of Nickie's criminal buddies had bailed him out. Antonio said it was just as well and seemed somewhat relieved. He said he had wanted to see Nickie so he could look him in the eyes and punch him in the face. Antonio had no doubt he would have ended up in jail with him.

"Let his degenerate friends take care of him! Let them deal with his problems! We have done all we can do."

They could hear the anger and frustration in Antonio's voice. It was obvious to them he was in a lot of pain and was trying not to show it. Shortly after, Antonio said he wasn't hungry and excused himself from dinner. He went upstairs, and they didn't see him again that night.

Josie and Sophia stayed downstairs and talked for hours. They had a lengthy conversation about Nickie that night and agreed he was heading for a life of crime. Josie knew Sophia was heartbroken over the choices Nickie had made in his life, but she had accepted the fact that they had done all they could do. They eventually went to bed.

# Chapter Five

Josie was awakened the next morning by Nickie tugging open the dresser drawers. He was pulling them out and throwing them on the floor. He took a suitcase from the closet and began cramming his clothes into it. He looked disheveled and was moving with great speed.

"What are you doing? Where are you going?" asked Josie.

"None of your business!" he shouted.

"Talk to me," she said.

"I'll talk to you. You are going to work when this baby is born," he commanded.

"Work? How can I work after I have a kid?" she asked.

"That's your problem," he said in a condescending tone.

There was a knock at the door, and it opened before she could say another word. It was Antonio. He began shouting at Nickie.

"You have outdone yourself this time. You have a lot of nerve coming here. Get out of this house! Now! You are not welcome here!"

"I came to get my things," said Nickie.

"Fine! Get them and get out!"

Josie was afraid the argument was going to end in a physical altercation. She could see the anger on Antonio's face, and it was clear to her he was making a special effort to control himself. He stood impatiently by the door, waiting for Nickie to finish packing. Nickie slammed his suitcase shut, latched it, and picked it up. He rushed past Antonio, pushing him aside, and hurried down the stairs.

Josie knew Antonio could see the fear on her face. He was concerned Nickie had hurt her.

"Are you okay?" asked Antonio with compassion.

"Yes, I'm fine," insisted Josie.

Antonio moved with great speed as he was obviously anxious to confront Nickie. He practically ran down the stairs after him. She could hear them yelling. Sophia came into her bedroom to comfort her. Josie would never forget Sophia's words that day.

"Nickie is a troubled boy. I'm afraid for you and the baby. You should get a divorce from him after the baby is born. It is hard for a mother to admit, but sometimes he scares me. You never know what he might do next. He is never going to change. He is our son, but we have no idea what to do with him. Quiet; let's listen."

Sophia wanted to hear what was going on downstairs. The only thing they heard was the slamming of the front door. Josie and Sophia heard Antonio's footsteps coming back up the stairs. They both scrambled so Antonio wouldn't know they had been trying to listen.

Antonio walked back into Josie's room.

"He's gone. I told him not to come back. We should go downstairs. Sophia can make us some coffee." Josie could hear the disgust in Antonio's voice.

They didn't hear from Nickie again. Josie was

certain Nickie knew Antonio wanted nothing more to do with him.

A couple of months passed. Things seemed normal. Josie told me it was nice not having to put up with Nickie's abusive behavior. However, there was a part of Josie that felt guilty and sometimes she wondered if she was the cause of the trouble between him and his parents. They continually reassured her that was not the case. They told her many stories of the problems they had with Nickie long before Josie got involved with him. Some of them were dreadful, but Josie was not at all surprised. She got to know him well in a short time and got to know some of his friends. They weren't respectable people.

Antonio went to Nickie's arraignment. He didn't think it would be good for Josie to go because of her pregnancy. He didn't want Sophia to go either, because he thought it would be too emotional for her. Regardless of how badly he behaved, Nickie was still her son. Antonio reluctantly went by himself.

When Antonio came home late that night, Josie and Sophia were anxious to hear how things went. Sophia poured tea for everyone, and they all gathered in the living room where most of the serious conversations took place. Antonio sat back in his rocking chair with a solemn look on his face. He went on to explain the events of the day.

"It is without question the outcome will not be good," said Antonio in a humbled voice.

"Exactly what does 'not good' mean?" asked Sophia.

"It means he will be pleading guilty to the charges and will probably have to spend some time in jail," said Antonio.

"How much time do you think he will have to spend?" asked Sophia.

Josie sat quietly and listened.

"If I had to guess, maybe five years. With good behavior, he may get out sooner," said Antonio.

Josie could hear Sophia weep. She reached over and placed her arm on Sophia's back and tried to comfort her. Afterward there was silence. No one mentioned it again. They were all still in a bit of shock.

None of Nickie's family went to his sentencing. Antonio and Sophia didn't want to be there to watch them take him away to jail. His brother Seth said he had to work, his sister Selena said she had to stay with the kids, and Josie told

Antonio she had no reason to go.

Officer Carl Simpson stopped by the house later that evening to update everyone. Josie and Sophia could hear Carl and Antonio talking outside. They overheard Officer Simpson say the judge sentenced Nickie to five years in jail. He and Antonio spoke a few minutes more, then Antonio went back into the house to tell Josie and Sophia the news. They tried to act surprised, because they didn't want him to know they had been listening. Antonio explained the details of Nickie's sentencing.

"He was sentenced to five years. He could get out in eighteen months with good behavior."

Antonio paused. She could tell he was trying to hold back the tears.

"Maybe it will do him some good. At least we will know where he is for a while," said Antonio.

"Nickie has always been in trouble. Most of his prior charges were misdemeanors, but even so, they didn't sit well with the judge at his sentencing. The judge expressed his concerns that he doesn't have faith that Nickie will stay out of trouble. He told the judge he wrote the bad checks to cover his gambling debts. He said he borrowed money from the wrong people, and they had given him a deadline to repay them. He said he was desperate and feared for his life. That didn't help his case either. The judge wasn't sympathetic," explained Antonio.

It seemed Antonio had prepared himself as much as he could. He stopped showing signs of anger or frustration. Sophia continued to cry off and on for days, but eventually she stopped. Josie would have been happy if they kept him for the full five years.

# Chapter

## Six

For a couple of months, everything was quiet. One morning, everyone went downstairs to the kitchen to have breakfast. Afterward, Sophia began clearing the table. Josie started sweeping the floor when her water broke. Josie was certain she had gone into labor. After much confusion, Sophia and Antonio managed to collect Josie's things and get everyone into the car. Antonio drove quickly to the county hospital. A few hours later, you were born. It was June 20, 1950.

Antonio called the jail and asked a guard to get a message to Nickie. He told the guard to let

Nickie know he had a daughter named Daniella. Antonio said he thought it was the right thing to do. Despite all that had happened, he still felt they should notify him. No one expected Nickie would have an interest in his child once he got out of prison, but they all knew he could be vindictive. They wanted to take the necessary steps to minimize the chance of him retaliating against Josie.

Josie mentioned that no one from our side of the family went to the hospital that day. I didn't have the heart to tell her our father had forbidden any of the family to go.

For Josie, living on her own had been difficult, but she adjusted to her new life as best she could. She would always love and cherish the family our father forced her to leave behind.

Later that day, the nurse came into the room and handed you to her. She said it was the most incredible feeling she had ever experienced. Although she still had much to worry about, for that moment, she feared nothing.

A few days later, Antonio and Sophia picked you and Josie up from the hospital. When they arrived back at the house, Antonio and Sophia told Josie to go directly upstairs. Josie said she opened the bedroom door and felt overwhelmed with tears of joy. Sophia and Antonio had spent hours preparing the room. A lace nightgown was lying on the bed for Josie, and a lovely baby's crib alongside her bed. There were small toys stacked on the chair and a baby blanket folded on the end of the dresser. Sophia had knitted several sweaters with matching booties for you. Josie wondered how she found time to make them. They were beautiful. It was a glorious sight.

The next week, Antonio and Sophia had a party for both of you. All the Demetrios family was there. They made Josie feel she was one of them. Some of her friends were even there. They spent hours celebrating and enjoying one another's company. They were all delighted to see you and Josie. Everyone seemed to be sincerely happy.

The next few months were great. Josie still worried about the future and feared the day Nickie would get out of jail. She knew it was only a matter of time before she would have to deal with him. She began to think a lot about a divorce but wondered where she would get the money. She also knew she couldn't live with Antonio and Sophia forever. Josie finally got the courage to bring up the subject.

"Sophia?"

"Yes, dear. What is it?"

"I've been thinking a lot about what we are going to do when Nickie gets out of prison."

Josie was afraid of how Sophia was going to handle both of you leaving someday. She was trying to be sensitive to Sophia's feelings.

"I don't understand." Sophia's voice began to break up. "You don't need to do anything."

"Yes, we do, Sophia. We can't live here forever. I also need to get a divorce. I certainly can't stay married to Nickie."

"I understand, dear. Antonio and I have talked about it. We agree that you should get a divorce. I guess now is as good a time as any. We know all of this has been very upsetting for you. We can see the worry on your face. It is better just to do it so you can get on with your life."

Josie said Sophia followed by telling her she didn't need to move. Josie began explaining why she couldn't continue to live with them.

"That's just it, Sophia. We can't. We cannot be here when Nickie gets out of prison. Please understand how much I love you and Antonio. You are the only family we have, and you have both been wonderful to us. I don't even know how we would get along without you. A day will come, we will need to figure it out. We have some time, and it's not something we have to deal with today."

There was silence. Josie and Sophia were both looking for a better solution, but they knew there wasn't one. The conversation with Sophia was difficult for Josie and it broke her heart to see the sadness on Sophia's face.

That night at the dinner table, the subject of divorce came up again. Only this time Antonio brought it up. Sophia sat quietly and listened.

"Josie, I understand you feel it would be best for you to file for a divorce from Nickie."

Josie thought for a second. Wanting to be gentle, she decided a simple, honest response was best.

"Yes, Antonio. I do."

"We understand. Sophia and I have talked about it and we agree. Sadly, we can understand why you wouldn't want to stay married to Nickie. I took the liberty of calling a family friend. He is a divorce lawyer and I am certain he can help. I explained the details of your situation and Dan said he would be happy to meet with you. Here's his name and telephone number. He will be in his office tomorrow and is expecting your call. You will need to schedule an appointment with him. We know you don't have any money, but we don't want you to worry. Sophia and I will pay for everything. We will take you to Dan's office when you need to go, and we will do everything we can to get you through this."

Josie could tell Antonio's conscience was bothering him. It was his son they were discussing. She was certain Antonio and Sophia knew Nickie was a troubled boy. She also knew they would have preferred she and Nickie had ended up happily married, but they knew there was no possibility of that ever happening. They also knew the only option was for them to get a divorce, so it was a bittersweet day for the family.

Josie called the lawyer's office the next day and scheduled an appointment. She was lucky enough to get one for late in the afternoon. Antonio and Sophia went with Josie to see the attorney, Dan Levinstein. His secretary escorted them into his office the moment they arrived.

Dan closed the door behind them. The attorney was a very tall, well-dressed, distinguished-looking man with salt and pepper hair. He wasn't particularly handsome, but you were certain to notice him when he walked into a room. Josie could tell he and Antonio had a long history and a mutual sense of respect.

"Please take a seat. Antonio, it's good to see you. I'm sorry it's under such unpleasant circumstances," he said.

"Likewise," replied Antonio.

Antonio pulled a chair back for Sophia.

"Hello, you must be Josie. I am Dan Levinstein. Antonio and I have been friends for as long as I can remember. We have discussed your situation, and I realize this must be a difficult time for you. I want to make this as easy as possible."

He spoke with compassion, and Josie felt comfortable with him within minutes. She sat directly in front of him and gave him her undivided attention.

"It's a relatively simple process. I'll have my staff draw up the papers and we'll have you sign them. Then we'll send someone over to get Nickie to sign them. However, we need to work out a few details. What about the issue of financial support? We need to consider visitation rights when he gets out of jail."

Josie said everyone in the room stared at her as they awaited her response. She was passionate in her delivery as she insisted she didn't want anything to do with Nickie.

"No! I don't want child support. I certainly don't want him to have visitation rights."

"Oh my, Josie. That's going to be difficult to do. He is the father, isn't he?" he asked.

She couldn't believe he would ask her such a question.

"Of course he's the father!"

"I'm sorry, Josie. I had to ask," he said apologetically. "It's almost impossible to stop a parent from seeing their child. Has he mistreated you in some way?" he asked.

Josie hesitated. She knew it would be best for everyone if she said no. She took a deep breath.

"No," she said reluctantly.

"You know, Josie, let's not try to deal with this now. Nickie is going to be in jail for a while, so we should wait until he gets out. We'll deal with it when we must. A lot could change by then. Fair enough?" he asked.

Sophia and Antonio were silent, allowing Josie to handle it.

"How long before the papers would be ready?" asked Josie.

"I need a couple of weeks," he said.

"A couple of weeks? That's much sooner than I expected." Josie was eager, but nervous.

"I think we can move quickly under the circumstances," replied Dan.

There was silence for a few minutes. Then they looked at one another, and it seemed they all knew everything they needed to know. Antonio stood up from his chair, and Josie and Sophia got up and thanked the attorney. They shook hands and said goodbye.

A couple of weeks later, Antonio received a telephone call from Dan Levinstein. The papers were ready to sign. Antonio drove Josie to his office. They walked in and she signed them. They spoke for a few minutes.

"We'll be sending someone over to serve Nickie within the next couple of days," said Dan.

It was a brief meeting. Once again, they thanked him and left.

A few days later, Antonio received a telephone call from Dan Levinstein. He had a lengthy conversation with him. After Antonio hung up, he shared the news with Sophia and Josie. He said Nickie had refused to sign the divorce papers. Antonio told Sophia and Josie that Dave, the process server, went to the jail to serve Nickie. He became enraged and threatened to inflict bodily harm. He said he would never sign the papers and threw them back at Dave. Dave reported that Nickie was so angry, the guard had to remove him from the room. He could hear Nickie yelling profanities as they began escorting him back to his cell.

Josie, Antonio, and Sophia sat for a while trying to figure out their next course of action. Antonio suggested Josie visit Nickie in jail and try to talk to him. She told him there was no way she was going there, because she was afraid of him. She insisted she couldn't face him again.

Dan also told Antonio that under the circumstances, Josie could get a divorce from Nickie without his signature or his consent, but Dan thought it would be best for Josie to try to convince him to cooperate. Josie was visibly frustrated, and she knew everyone could tell she was not interested in going to the jail to see Nickie. That was the last thing she would ever want to do. Her greatest dream was never to see him again.

After several hours of discussion, there didn't seem to be a better solution. Josie needed to try to get Nickie's approval. She knew if she didn't, she would pay a price in the end. Josie reconsidered the possibility of going to the jail, since she knew there would be a guard there to protect her. Finally, but reluctantly, she agreed. Antonio called Dan and told him of their decision, and Dan said he would make the arrangements.

# Chapter Seven

$\mathcal{S}$ hortly after, Josie got the courage to go to the jail to visit Nickie. She asked Antonio to take her. They had a discussion in the car about the best way to handle the meeting. The one thing they both agreed on was that Josie would have to speak to Nickie alone.

When they arrived at the jail, Josie and Antonio went through the standard procedure to check in. Antonio positioned himself in a seat in the waiting area. A few minutes later, they called Josie's name, and a guard came out to escort her. Josie felt queasy as they walked down a very long hallway to get to the visitors' room. She knew they had arrived when she saw an armed guard standing by the door. The guard opened the door, took her inside, and sat her at the visitors' table in the center of the room. Barely four feet separated her and the chair where Nickie would sit. For her, it wasn't far enough. Josie was certain she was visibly nervous.

Josie was there for only a few minutes before the guard brought Nickie into the room. They escorted him to the table where she sat. Josie couldn't help but notice they had restrained Nickie with shackles. The guard pulled back a chair directly in front of her. She watched Nickie maneuver into the seat as he tried to make himself comfortable. When he placed his hands on the table in front of her, she was relieved to see he was wearing handcuffs.

It had been months since Josie had seen him. He was thin and frail, and he looked tired and worn. His eyes were full of rage. He glared at her for a couple of minutes with the obvious intention of intimidating her. She sat for a few moments with her head down, contemplating what to say.

"What are you doing here, Josie?" he asked.

Josie was careful to speak calmly.

"We need to talk."

Nickie twisted and turned in his chair. She knew he wanted to make her feel uncomfortable. She had to be very careful what she said to him, because she didn't want to enrage him.

"We have nothing to talk about."

Josie could see the anger on his face. She spoke quietly to try not to make him angrier.

"Yes, Nickie, we do. We need to talk about getting a divorce," she said.

"Divorce! We're not getting a divorce. I don't want a divorce," he declared.

Nickie had always been unpredictable. Josie never knew what his next move would be. Even though there was an armed guard at the door, she still sat across from him in fear.

"I don't understand, Nickie. Why wouldn't you want to get a divorce? It doesn't make sense," she argued.

"We'll get a divorce when I am ready!"

She could tell jail had made him even more obstinate than he was before.

"Don't even think about trying to take my kid away! Bitch, you can't be that crazy! You know better than to try to take Daniella away from me. It will be the last thing you ever do. Do you understand?"

He looked straight into her eyes and glared at her. She could see his anger. He was threatening and convincing.

"Do you, Josie? Do you understand, or do I need to explain it to you?"

His voice was escalating. He stood from his chair and kicked it backward.

"Leave now! Don't come here again!" he shouted.

The guard rushed over to him.

"Calm down," said the guard.

The guard had a grave look on his face, and Josie sensed his concern.

"You need to leave now. This visit is over," declared the guard. He began pulling Nickie away from the chair and started dragging him out of the room.

"That's right, bitch! Leave, and don't come back."

Nickie continued to struggle with the guard.

"Remember what I said, Josie. I won't let you take my kid. If you try, you will live to regret it."

Josie told me he scowled at her and turned to

the guard and began shouting.

"That's right! You heard me. She'll live to regret it."

From the defiant look on his face, it was obvious to Josie that he feared nothing.

"Please leave," insisted the guard. "Let's go, Nickie. Now! That's enough."

Another guard rushed in and grabbed Nickie by his other arm. Nickie began shouting profanities at Josie. Josie could hear him continue to yell as they removed him from the room. She practically ran down the hall and back into the waiting room. Josie saw Antonio sitting in a chair and rushed toward him. He saw her coming through the door and stood to greet her. Josie broke down into tears. She was shaking.

"He's crazy! It was a mistake coming here. Nickie's gone mad. How could I possibly think I could reason with a madman?"

Josie was crying so hard Antonio could barely understand her.

"Why doesn't he want to get a divorce?"

Josie was panic-stricken.

"Antonio! What will I do?" she cried.

"I don't know, dear. It's a control issue with

Nickie. He always wants to be in control. Let's go home and we'll talk about it later. Come on. Let's get you home."

As he always did, Antonio showed compassion toward Josie. He placed his arms around her and held her gently. They walked briskly to the car. Antonio opened the car door for her, so she could get in. He fastened her seat belt and made certain it was secure. She cried all the way home.

When they got home, Antonio and Sophia tried to comfort Josie. Unfortunately, there wasn't much anyone could do to change her mood. Josie fixated on her dilemma and her mind raced as she contemplated many possibilities. None seemed to solve her problem. Josie knew Nickie was a cruel man and she knew she would pay the price if she opposed him.

They sat at the table for hours rehashing the story. Josie told them she knew Nickie would never grant her a divorce unless he decided he was ready. It was clear to everyone Josie had no alternative but to get a divorce without Nickie's consent. Josie wasn't happy knowing one day she would have to face Nickie. She feared what would happen when she finally did see him again. She prayed she could disappear by the time he got out of prison, but she feared that no matter where she went, he would find her.

Antonio called Dan Levinstein and told him about Josie's visit with Nickie. Antonio said they discussed it in detail and had decided a divorce without Nickie's consent was the only logical way to go.

Dan agreed with the family's decision and committed to making the arrangements. He said he would let them know when the divorce would be final. Within a few months, they received the papers by certified mail. Josie said there was a part of her that felt relieved. She had just separated herself from Nickie, at least on paper, but she wasn't foolish enough to think it was over. She knew she had just entered a war with a psychopath.

At the time of the divorce, you had just turned six months old. It was the week of Christmas 1950. You both celebrated the holidays with the Demetrios family. The house was beautifully decorated for the season. The entire Demetrios family was there for Christmas dinner. No one mentioned Nickie's name, to Josie's relief.

Josie said 1951 was her first peaceful year.

Then in January 1952, she got the news. Nickie would get out of prison within a few months. Josie felt anxious. She knew she would have to move before he got out. Even Antonio and Sophia thought it was best. Where would she go? What would she do for money? Those were only a few of the things that concerned her.

Everyone agreed you and Josie should stay at Antonio and Sophia's best friend's house for a while. Jim and Julia Armento lived only a few miles from them. Everyone was confident Nickie wouldn't look for her there. Josie packed a few things and moved into their home a few weeks later. Since they were all very concerned Nickie may have someone watching Antonio and Sophia's house, they took as many precautions as possible. They had to move quickly. No one completely understood why Nickie was going to come looking for you and Josie. They just knew he would. There was no logical reason for anything he did.

Antonio gave Josie some money. He wanted to make sure she was financially secure. He and Sophia thought she had enough to worry about without having to worry about finances. Everyone agreed it would be best to limit visits for a while.

They wanted to wait and see what state of mind Nickie was in when he got out of jail. Josie wouldn't have minded if they kept Nickie longer. Time had gone by too quickly for her. She was sad to leave Antonio and Sophia and her comfortable surroundings. Unfortunately, she understood the need to find a safe place where Nickie couldn't find either of you.

# Chapter Eight

For months everything was quiet. The Armentos were kind and compassionate. Their two-story home was beautiful and spacious. The furniture was all high-end traditional. They were art collectors, and you couldn't help but notice the exceptional original paintings that lined the walls of each of the rooms. They had five bedrooms and three bathrooms. There was more than enough space for Josie and you.

The Armentos were a lovely elderly couple. They tried hard to make Josie feel at home. She felt comfortable living there, but she missed her family and Nickie's parents. It was one of the loneliest times she had ever experienced. Josie was afraid of what the future would hold. There didn't seem to be a light at the end of the tunnel. She believed there was some good that came out of it. You were the one thing that would be constant in her life.

As everyone expected, Josie found out Nickie was looking for both of you.

Antonio called Jim Armento.

"He was here, and we are worried. He was much worse than we expected. I don't understand. Why can't he leave them alone? Is Josie close to the phone?" he asked.

"Yes, she's right here," said Jim.

Jim handed Josie the telephone.

"Hi, Josie. How are my girls?" he asked lovingly.

"Fine, Antonio. What's up? Something's wrong. I can tell."

"You're right. Nickie was here looking for you and he was furious."

Antonio began speaking rapidly as he shared the details of Nickie's visit.

"Nickie stormed into the house and demanded to know where you and Daniella were. He looked out of sorts, like he might have been high on something."

Antonio said he and Sophia were both shocked at his demeanor. He was very confrontational, and they both felt threatened by his behavior.

"He is our son, but he frightens us. He is out of control." Antonio's voice was trembling as he related the scene that occurred:

"What are you doing here?" asked Antonio.

"Where's Josie? Where's my kid?" He demanded an answer.

"Nickie, why don't you leave them alone? What are they to you? You don't care anything about them," said Antonio.

Antonio said Nickie got less than a foot from his face and began shouting.

"Who are you to tell me what I care about or what is important to me? Where are they? Tell me now!" he demanded.

"Are you threatening me?" asked Antonio. "Don't ever come here with that tone of voice and threaten me!"

Antonio said Nickie was disrespectful to them. Sophia was beginning to get very upset as tempers flared.

"Please leave, Nickie!" insisted Antonio.

At that point, Antonio said Sophia wanted him out of the house.

"This isn't doing anyone any good. You know we wouldn't tell you if we knew," said Sophia.

"You need to get a hold of yourself, or you are going to end up back in jail," said Antonio.

"You don't know what you're saying. I'm not going back to jail," Nickie shouted. He began rushing up the stairs.

Antonio said he rushed behind Nickie and placed his hand on Nickie's arm. Nickie shoved Antonio backward. Antonio said Sophia ran into the kitchen and picked up the telephone. She began dialing. Nickie stopped for a moment on the stairs.

"Who are you calling?" yelled Nickie.

"I'm calling the police," she said.

Antonio said he began trying to get Nickie to leave the house. At first, he asked. Then he demanded that Nickie leave.

"I won't tolerate this type of behavior in our home! You can't just come here and push and shove your way around. I won't allow it!"

Nickie yelled at his mother to put down the

phone.

"Only if you leave now!" she said.

"All right! I'll leave, but I'm going to find them. I will find them with or without your help!"

Antonio said Nickie glared at them with fire in his eyes. He finally turned and stormed out of the house. They heard him slam his car door and squeal his tires down the street.

"We are afraid for you and the baby. Nickie is on a rampage. We are fearful of what he might do. We love you both. Please be careful. We don't want to frighten you, but he is really in a bad place right now. He is not rational. We'll let you know if we hear anything more from him," he said.

"Thanks for the warning."

Josie hung up the phone and asked the Armentos what they should do.

"Nothing, dear," said Jim. "He doesn't know you're staying here. We should remain calm."

"I guess you're right. No need to panic," said Josie.

The days went by slowly. Josie said she lived in fear. She knew she was in danger but had no idea how much. She looked over her shoulder every place she went. Most of the time she stayed at home because she was afraid to go out.

The Armentos decided to go to the market that following Saturday. Josie wanted to stay behind so she could take her time getting both of you dressed. The Armentos wanted to take you both to a nice lunch in town later in the day.

Josie thought she heard an unusual noise when she was walking upstairs. She turned and went back downstairs to the living room, wondering if the Armentos had forgotten something. She waited, but no one came in. She walked over and slowly opened the front door.

She looked to her left. Nickie was standing firmly against the wall. He turned and grabbed her by the throat with great speed and force. She thought for sure he would choke her to death. She began gasping for air. She tried to scream, but she couldn't. Nickie had his hands tightly around her throat.

"You bitch! I told you not to take my kid. I told you if you did you would pay. Did you think I wouldn't find you?"

She told me he was meaner and angrier than she had ever seen him. She said she knew she would get only one chance. So, using every bit of force she had, she kicked him between the legs. He let out a yell that she felt sure the entire neighborhood could hear. He crouched over and then he looked up at her. She could see the pain in his face and his eyes were full of rage. She knew he wasn't going to quit until he had severely injured her or worse. She caught her breath and began screaming at the top of her lungs.

"Help me! Someone, please! Help me! He's trying to kill me!"

He got his second wind. She started to run, but he grabbed her before she could get away. She knew she was fighting for her life. She kicked, screamed, and fought back with all the strength she had left. There was an enormous struggle. As she turned toward the street, she could see someone rushing out of a house. At that moment, Nickie pushed her. She tumbled down the front steps, feeling the force of every step. When she reached the bottom, she landed on her back and could feel pain radiate down her spine. She tried to get up, but she couldn't move. She could hear someone running toward her. She heard Nickie's footsteps as he took off running through the yard. Someone was yelling.

"The police are on the way."

Josie didn't recognize the voice. She didn't remember anything afterward. Everything went dark. She lay unconscious on the ground. An ambulance came and transported her to a nearby hospital. Josie regained consciousness for a few moments when she was inside the ambulance. She begged for someone to hide you from Nickie. She later found out a neighbor had gone upstairs to your bedroom and gotten you. You stayed with them until the Armentos came home.

For two days, Josie went in and out of consciousness. Both of her eyes were black and blue, and she had bruises all over her body. She had a shattered collarbone, a dislocated hip, and two broken ribs. She had several internal injuries and a concussion. She was a mess, but she was alive.

Josie said Antonio and Sophia visited her in the hospital. They sat by her bed. A couple of times Josie regained consciousness, and she could hear Antonio weeping.

"Nickie will pay for this, Josie. I promise you. He will pay for this."

Josie stayed in the hospital for the next two months. She went through endless hours of surgery and rehabilitation. There was a policeman posted outside of her room every minute of every day.

Nickie was in a lot of trouble. He had violated his probation and the police had issued a warrant for his arrest.

Janice, one of the Demetrios's neighbors, came forward. She told the police officers that she'd heard tires squealing that day. She looked outside and saw a car speeding from down the street. She realized it was Nickie Demetrios's car. She watched him as he parked in front of her house. He stepped out of his car and took off running through the yard behind hers. She considered calling the police, but she always thought he was a little crazy.

Janice continued to watch Nickie jumping the fences and racing through the backyards. He was moving with great speed. He reached his parents' home and slowly crept up the back steps of the house. She watched him walk over and stand firmly against the back wall. Nickie leaned in close to the window. He appeared to be trying to see or hear what was going on inside. He stood there for a few minutes before he walked slowly and quietly down the back steps of the Demetrios home. Janice watched him walk briskly between the houses to his car. He got in and sped away.

Janice didn't think much more about it until she later heard what had happened to Josie. She figured out that must have been how Nickie found out where Josie was staying. Janice regretted she hadn't called Antonio or the police. She felt terrible she didn't do something. She thought if she had, it might have prevented what had happened to Josie.

Antonio told the officers he had called Josie at Jim's house to warn her right after Nickie took off from the house. He said he was on the telephone in the kitchen. If Nickie was at the back of the house, Antonio was sure Nickie could have heard him speaking. Antonio remembered calling Jim by his name on several occasions. There was no doubt in anyone's mind that was when Nickie realized you and Josie were staying with the Armentos.

When it was time for Josie to leave the hospital, she realized she had nowhere to go. Everyone agreed she couldn't go back to the Armentos. The Armentos said they had friends where both of you could stay. Josie decided to accept their offer. She agreed to stay there for a couple of weeks until she could figure something out.

You had just celebrated your third birthday. Josie had become very protective of you. She knew she couldn't let Nickie find you. Josie said your safety was all that mattered. She knew she needed to find a safe place to hide but worried there wasn't such a place. Nickie had always been resourceful. She knew he had friends who would help him hunt her down, causing her to live every day in fear. She wondered how many more times she would have to move.

# Chapter Nine

The healing process was slow. Most of the time, Josie was in a lot of pain. She had several operations on her shoulder. Eventually, the doctors decided the only way to repair it was with metal pins and a plate. The surgeries left a terrible scar, not only physically but also emotionally. Josie had always been afraid of Nickie, but now she felt terrified. The harsh reality had set in. He was even more dangerous than she had originally thought. Josie was sincerely afraid for you. She contemplated a lot of questions. Would he steal you? Was he evil enough to hurt you? Was that how he would get his revenge? What was next? Josie knew it was far from over. Nickie would never give up until he found both of you.

For the next few months, Josie moved around a lot. She lived with more than six of the Armentos' friends. They were kind enough to let you both stay with them. Josie didn't want to wear out her welcome or risk placing anyone else in danger. She didn't want to take a chance Nickie would find out where you were, so she was always moving. She thought the more she moved around, the more difficult it would be for Nickie to catch up with her. She tried to stay one step ahead of him, but she was running out of places to go. Running and hiding became more exhausting each day. She was beginning to feel ill, and was certain she couldn't take another step, but she pressed forward.

One afternoon, the telephone rang. It was Antonio.

"Josie, the police located Nickie. He is in police custody. They have arrested him."

"Thank goodness," said Josie.

Josie and Antonio shared a sigh of relief.

"They have taken statements from the neighbors that witnessed his assault on you. He will be going back to jail for some time. At least for now, Josie, he is not a threat to you or Daniella. I will let you know as soon as I find out more."

Josie said she couldn't have been happier. She expressed her feelings to Antonio for all he and Sophia had done for her.

"Thank you for everything, Antonio. I can only imagine how hard all of this must be on you and Sophia."

She felt an enormous amount of love for them.

"Don't worry about us, Josie. Worry about yourself and Daniella. We will take care of the rest. My concern for you has always taken priority over everything else, including my son."

Antonio and Sophia told Josie about a lady who could use some help. Her name was Mrs. Jacobson. Her husband had died many years before, and she was sickly and alone. At that point, Josie was open to suggestions. She was hopeful something would finally work out. Sophia mentioned you and Josie to Mrs. Jacobson. She invited you both to stay with her. Josie immediately began packing and within a few days, you moved in. Josie was happy she would be able to settle in for a while at least. The events of the past months had taken a toll on her.

Josie liked Mrs. Jacobson the minute she met her. She dressed nicely, even at her age. Mrs. Jacobson was smart, worldly, and sophisticated. She was thin, pale, and fragile. Mrs. Jacobson had straight white teeth and a lovely smile. Josie could tell she must have been a beautiful young woman. Mrs. Jacobson was exceptionally kind. Her home was small but lavishly decorated. Josie and Mrs. Jacobson got along well, and Josie enjoyed taking care of her. Mrs. Jacobson was grateful to have you both stay and considered you and Josie family.

Josie continued to meet with Antonio and Sophia in the park occasionally for lunch. While she thought things seemed to be working out well for her, there was one thing Josie knew for certain. Nothing lasts forever. She was about to get news that would drastically change your lives.

She said Nickie's older brother Seth rarely called. On this day, he did. Josie had a terrible ache in her stomach and feared the worst. She could hear his voice quiver and knew Seth was about to share some bad news.

"Yes, Seth. What is it?"

She anxiously awaited his response. He began to sob so hard Josie couldn't understand him. Selena got on the telephone.

"Josie, there's been a terrible accident."

Selena's voice was trembling.

"What is it? What's wrong?" pleaded Josie.

Josie told me it was one of the worst days of her life.

"It's bad, Josie. Antonio and Sophia were killed in an automobile accident," cried Selena.

"What do you mean? I don't understand!"

Josie was in shock.

"That's impossible!" she exclaimed.

"A drunk driver hit their car on their way home from an evening outing with friends. The car hit a tree going an estimated fifty-five miles an hour. It spun out of control and went off a cliff. They were both killed instantly," cried Selena.

Josie screamed in anguish.

"How can this be? We spent the day with them in the park yesterday. It was a beautiful day! We had a great time together. How can this be?"

"I know, Josie. I know." Selena continued sobbing. "If you like, we'll come by to pick you up," said Selena.

"Of course," said Josie. "We'll be ready when you get here."

You were upstairs taking your nap. Mrs. Jacobson was in her room sleeping. Josie walked into your bedroom and sat in the chair by your bed. She stared out the bedroom window, unable to move. She could hear the doorbell ring several times and finally got the strength to go downstairs to answer it. She could see through the peephole it was Selena and Seth and opened the door. They all grabbed onto one another and sobbed continuously. Seth was too upset to speak. Josie tried to be strong for them, but she couldn't help herself and cried uncontrollably.

"I didn't want to wake Daniella until you got here," said Josie.

"That's fine," said Selena.

"Please make yourselves comfortable. Give me a few minutes and I'll bring Daniella downstairs. I also need to tell Mrs. Jacobson what happened," said Josie.

"Of course. That's a good idea. We'll wait here," said Selena.

Seth sat on the sofa and was unable to contain himself. He continued to sob quietly.

Antonio and Seth had been very close. It was truly a sad day for all of you.

Nickie's parents had been kind and generous to Josie. They were what kept her going. They not only helped her financially, but they also helped her emotionally. Their love gave her strength and courage. She couldn't imagine what life was going to be like without them.

As Josie helped with the necessary arrangements to lay Antonio and Sophia to rest, she began to feel the stress of burying two people she had grown to love. She was grief-stricken and became violently ill at the viewing. She was unable to attend the funeral.

Just when she thought things couldn't get worse, they did. Josie suffered another loss a few weeks after the burial of Antonio and Sophia. She went upstairs one morning to bring Mrs. Jacobson her breakfast and found her dead in her bed. It was without warning. She had gone to sleep the night before and never woken up. Many people thought the events of the previous few weeks had been too much for her. She hadn't been the same since her husband died. Now she had lost Antonio and Sophia. They had been friends for more than twenty years and she loved them deeply. Once again, Josie made the necessary arrangements to bury a loved one.

Afterward, Josie went into a deep depression and could hardly get out of bed. She said Selena and Seth came over for a few days to help her pack. Josie knew once they finished helping her, she was on her own. There were many things she would have to figure out by herself. She knew she would have to leave Mrs. Jacobson's home soon, but she had no place to go. Now what?

Josie would lie in bed morning, noon, and night, staring at the ceiling. She said it felt like she was in a catatonic state. She would get up to feed and bathe you and go back to bed. She spent most of her time sleeping. She knew she had to pull herself together. The only thing that kept her going was knowing that you needed her, and she knew she had to take care of you.

Then one day she got up and put on her best dress. After asking a neighbor to take care of you, she began driving around. Josie stopped at a restaurant for a cup of coffee and sat quietly thinking about what she could do to make enough money to take care of both of you. She hadn't graduated high school and she didn't have any work experience. A waitress came to her table and asked if she would like a refill. That's when it occurred to her to become a waitress.

Josie said she thought for a second. What about the restaurant she was in drinking coffee? It was a busy restaurant and was intimidating. She was sure the restaurant would need someone with experience. She paid her bill and got back into her car and drove from restaurant to restaurant looking for a waitress job. She looked frantically day after day. It took weeks, but she finally found someone desperate enough to hire her. She began working as a waitress in a cute little café a thirty-minute drive from Mrs. Jacobson's home.

The neighbors were kind and would take turns taking care of you. Josie would pick you up after work and go home to fix you dinner. She worked hard and the tips were fair. She began to save every penny. Josie counted her money again and again. She knew she would need enough to rent an apartment, so she kept a ledger to make sure she didn't waste a cent.

Mrs. Jacobson's lawyer called Josie to let her know the house would be going on the market soon.

Josie began searching for a place where both of you could live. She couldn't afford much. She found an efficiency apartment close to the café where she worked. The walls were bare, and the kitchen had a refrigerator that was older than Josie. Two of the four burners on the stove worked. The bathroom only had a shower, and the bedroom had a double bed with a dresser at the foot of the bed. It certainly wasn't as nice as the places she had been living, but she convinced herself she could make it livable. At that point, she didn't have a choice. She had run out of places to go.

Mrs. Jacobson's neighbors donated tons of items to help Josie set up her new home. Seth and Selena helped her with all the work. They managed to repair everything that was broken, helped paint the walls and a few pieces of furniture. They hung the pictures and put the furniture in its place. After they finished everything, they stopped to admire their hard work. It was cute, in an odd sort of way. Everything was clean and painted, and it didn't matter to Josie that nothing matched. Josie, Seth, and Selena went back to Mrs. Jacobson's to finish packing her things, and then Seth and Selena helped her move everything into the new place.

Josie was worried, because she still had a lot of things she needed to work out. Who would take care of you while she worked? She knew she could continue to take you to Mrs. Jacobson's neighbors for a while, but she also knew she would eventually need to find someone closer to her new apartment.

Josie had cried every day after Antonio, Sophia, and Mrs. Jacobson died. Then one day, she stopped. Josie wondered why she hadn't cried since. She thought for certain she must have run out of tears.

# Chapter Ten

osie was forced to stop mourning her losses. There wasn't time. Her concerns about the future were beginning to take a toll on her. For a while, everything was out of sync. Survival was what drove her. It was like being in the ocean way over your head, with the tide taking you farther and farther out. Your survival instincts kick in and push you to keep going. There were many times she thought for certain she would drown. All she could see was you drowning with her, and she wasn't going to let that happen. She felt frustrated and had no patience with you or anyone else. She kept moving forward and as time went on, she got tougher.

Gradually, things started to get better. Josie invited a friend who worked with her at the café to come over to the apartment for dinner. Her name was Gina and she was beautiful. Josie described her as looking as if she were someone from an exotic foreign country. She had prominent features, long black wavy hair, and dark brown eyes. Gina had a laugh that was unbelievably contagious. Josie wasn't always sure why Gina was laughing, but she always laughed with her.

The first time Gina came to visit, they sat up most of the night talking. Josie enjoyed her company. It had been a long time since she had a reason to smile. Josie and Gina spent hours getting to know each other. They talked about most everything, but Josie thought it was odd Gina never mentioned her family. Josie thought she would eventually talk about them, but she never did. She believed it was best not to ask. She knew there was a story but didn't want to pry. She didn't want to take a chance she might upset Gina. After that night, Josie and Gina became good friends, and the three of you became a family.

Josie and Gina saw each other at work and

often hung out together afterward. Sometimes they went on double dates. Josie said they were enjoying each other's company. For the first time in years, Josie was embracing life. Sometimes when they worked different shifts, Gina stayed with you. She was always eager to help.

Then you got very sick. They were both worried and took you to the doctor. The doctor told Josie you were having migraine headaches. He prescribed medication. It would help you sleep, but when you woke up you had the same violent headache. You began throwing up most everything you ate, and you started losing too much weight. You cried continuously. It was hard for Josie and Gina to see you in pain. One night they rushed you to the hospital. The doctors ran even more tests and agreed you were having migraines. They prescribed a different medication, but nothing changed. The same thing would happen. You would go to sleep and wake up in excruciating pain. You often needed medical attention. The doctors told Josie your migraines would most likely go away when you got older.

The doctor bills and hospital bills were beginning to pile up. Josie was getting deeper into debt. Then she got behind on the rent. Her landlord was a kind and sensitive man. He had a big heart and showed a lot of compassion. He tried to be patient. Unfortunately, he had bills he needed to pay. He had no choice but to serve Josie with an eviction notice. She had to move out. Having very little money, she searched for several weeks for something affordable. The only apartment Josie could find was a run-down efficiency in a bad part of town. She said it looked like a cheap hotel room and the neighborhood was very scary.

Josie said the stress was beginning to take a toll on her. She had many obstacles to overcome. She lived in a seedy neighborhood where she feared for your safety. Josie knew she needed to work in a nice restaurant where she could make better tips. She had more experience than she'd had when she started. Unfortunately, there weren't any nice restaurants nearby. She needed to stay close to home to be near you, in case you had a migraine episode. Her car was old, and she often had trouble getting it started. She needed a new one.

Gina could tell Josie was on the verge of a nervous breakdown. Several months later, Gina suggested they get an apartment together. This way, they could both afford a bigger place. They moved into a large two-bedroom apartment in a better part of town. They found waitress jobs in a fancy restaurant where they could make better tips. The restaurant was close to their new place. They were very excited that things were looking up.

After they moved into the new apartment, they both worked long hours. They were home for only a few hours each day. You spent most of your time with babysitters. Josie would come back to the apartment and find you sleeping on the floor, freezing. The sitter would be lying on the couch asleep, bundled up in a nice warm blanket. One babysitter was always eating all the groceries. She was a large woman, but they still found it hard to believe that anyone could consume that much food in one night. They thought she was taking the groceries home. One babysitter was on the telephone all night talking to her boyfriend. Another ran up enormous long-distance phone bills. It was expensive, frustrating, and upsetting for both Josie and Gina. Josie said there were a lot of babysitters and none of them worked out for very long.

One night she went to check on you when she got home, and you weren't in your bed. She walked frantically through the house trying to find you. Josie found the babysitter sleeping in her bed. She had fallen asleep watching television. Josie said you were laying on the floor, dirty and hungry. There was no question in her mind that the sitter hadn't taken care of you that night.

Josie started bathing you before she left for work. Then she would put you in your bed. She would turn the light out in your room with the hope that you would fall asleep.

Josie often came home late at night. She would go into your room and look in on you. She would tuck the blanket around you and kiss you on the forehead. Josie was always fearful something bad had happened to you. She was beginning to feel the pressure of trying to be a working mother.

Josie didn't seem to think there was a way for her to work and keep you with her. She and Gina worked long hours and they were trying to save money. Josie decided she needed to leave you someplace where you would receive proper care. She started leaving you at different homes of people who specialized in caring for children. Most of the children they took care of belonged to unwed working mothers. It wasn't easy for Josie to leave you, but she didn't know what else to do because she was struggling to survive.

Josie would leave you for weeks, sometimes for months. You stayed in eight different homes that year. Some homes were nicer than others. It was unsettling for you, Josie, and Gina. It turned out to be another challenging year for Josie.

It was 1954. You were a few months away from your fourth birthday. Josie didn't want to leave you anymore. She and Gina decided they wanted to try again to keep you with them. For a brief time, they moved you back into the apartment to live with them.

Occasionally, male friends came over. They rarely visited for very long and they never stayed the night. Both Gina and your mother agreed they would never allow that to happen. They would just hang out and have fun. Their friends always left before it got to be too late.

Everything seemed to be going fine. Then one night, Josie brought a new friend named Danny home with her. She had only known him for a few weeks. Josie knew he'd had a lot to drink before they got to the apartment, but he seemed to be able to handle his liquor. He started talking loudly, and

Josie kept asking him to lower his voice. She began getting upset, because she didn't want him to wake you.

"My kid is sleeping!"

He mumbled something. Josie told him he needed to settle down. Otherwise, he was going to have to leave.

Josie excused herself and went to the bathroom. She came out a few minutes later and couldn't find him. At first, she thought he had left. Then Josie could hear his voice coming from your room. She could see him sitting on your bed. Josie started to panic. She couldn't understand why he was in there with you. Josie charged toward the room and saw him leaning over you. He began running his hands through your hair. She heard him mumble the same thing a couple of times: "Pretty girl."

Josie said she felt horrified. She watched him lean in and kiss you on the cheek. You turned your head and he grabbed your face and turned it toward him. He held it tightly and kissed you on the lips. Josie said it happened within seconds. She yelled at him at the top of her lungs as she continued to charge toward him. She looked over at you and you didn't move. You were frozen from fear.

"Danny! What are you doing!" Josie kept shouting at him. "What are you doing? What are you doing in my daughter's room? Don't touch her!"

She told me she began hitting him. She started punching him as hard as she could. He grabbed her hands and held them. He was muscular and overpowering. She couldn't break away.

"What? I was just looking!"

"Sure you were." Josie started crying.

By then you were crying and screaming. The only light in the room was coming from down the hall.

"Did he hurt you?"

You were incoherent.

"Daniella! Did he hurt you?"

Josie heard the front door open. Then she heard footsteps coming in her direction. It was Gina.

"What's going on in here? What's wrong? Tell me, Josie!" she pleaded.

Josie said she kept yelling at Danny to leave. You were crying. Danny was shouting at her and cursing. He began shaking Josie with force. Danny and Josie continued to struggle. Gina jumped in and started hitting him, but even together Gina and

Josie were no match for Danny. He could have easily held them both down.

Gina yelled at Josie, "Stop, Josie! Call the police."

"No! I am not going to call the cops. Just get him out of here. Please, Gina! Help me get him out of here!"

She and Gina pounded on him until he gave up. He finally took off. He went out the front door and slammed it behind him. Josie rushed over to lock it and then ran back into the room. You all grabbed onto one another, crying and trembling.

They kept asking you if he hurt you. You were too hysterical to respond. It took time for the three of you to calm down. Eventually you did, and they tucked you back into your bed. You were still afraid, so they left the light on for you. A short time later, you cried yourself to sleep.

The next day, Josie couldn't find a sitter. She had to go to work. Josie shared her frustration with Gina and then had a complete breakdown. She got angry. Josie was standing in the kitchen. She picked up cups and dishes and started throwing them. She begged Gina to do something.

"Please, Gina! I can't go on this way. It's too

much! Something needs to change! I can't do this anymore!"

Josie held her hands over her face and slid down the wall. Gina got down on the floor with her and tried to comfort her. Gina told her she knew someone who could help. At the time, Josie had no idea what Gina meant when she made that statement. Josie was exhausted and desperate. That was the day she made the worst decision she had ever made. She could never have imagined that your lives would never be the same.

Josie thought when she and Gina became friends that her life was getting better. Gina had great survival instincts. She was smart and resourceful. There is no doubt that Josie's love of Gina contributed to Josie's trust of her.

Gina's previous life remained a mystery to Josie. Even after all their time together, Gina never spoke about where she had come from or where she had been. Looking back, I think Josie regretted that she didn't learn more about Gina before agreeing to accept her help. Josie never recovered from the terrible decision she made on that day.

I know how much you loved Gina and I know she loved you and Josie, but I can't help but wonder how things would have turned out if she had not come into your lives.

It certainly didn't help that our father disowned Josie. She was young when our father threw her out of the house. She wasn't experienced enough to make good choices. She needed love and guidance. Instead, she was sent away to take care of the both of you on her own.

Our father was a good man and he had a beautiful heart, but nothing like that had ever happened to us before. He was shattered by the events and didn't know how to deal with them. He had allowed his anger and frustration to control him. I know he felt what he was doing was best for the family. However, our family was never the same after that night. Those events lived on in our lives and our hearts forever. They had a tremendously negative impact on our family union. If our father would have had the chance to do it over, I believe he would have done it differently. I don't think any of us ever forgave him for his decision.

There is no question that Josie made bad choices in her life, but she paid dearly for them. She struggled for years trying to do the best she could for both of you. She ran out of options. I don't think our father had any idea the toll his decision had taken on yours and Josie's lives. I know it would have devastated him if he ever found out.

# Chapter Eleven

*S* pringtime was always Josie's favorite time of the year. It was comfortable to go outside day or night. There was always a gentle breeze, and it seemed to have a calming effect on her.

Josie arranged for a sitter for you for a few hours, so she and Gina could go downtown and meet Gina's friends for lunch. Gina's friends seemed sincere and supportive. They reassured Josie not to worry and told her they would take care of everything. Everyone stayed and talked for a couple of hours, and then Josie and Gina headed back home.

Josie was up early the next morning. She left the house before anyone awoke. Gina stayed behind to take care of you.

Later that afternoon, Josie charged into the front door when she arrived back at the apartment. She was gushing with joy. She had a smile like none she'd ever had before. She was wearing cute little short shorts, a stretch scarf top, and white socks with sneakers. Her hair looked like she hadn't combed it in days. Josie held her arm up high in the air rattling keys and blurted out joyously:

"Look! Look what I have!"

Gina was in the kitchen making lunch. She came from around the corner with much enthusiasm.

She cried out, "You got it!"

"Oh yeah!"

Gina was happy. They finally had a reliable car. They grabbed each other and danced crazily around the room.

"What did you get, Mommy?"

"We got a new car. It isn't just any car. It is a beautiful white Cadillac Eldorado convertible with a red leather interior."

Josie was excited.

"Hurry! I want to show you."

Gina picked you up on her way out. Josie swung opened the screen door, and she and Gina enthusiastically rushed outside to see their new car. It was magnificent. It was long and sleek. The top was down. It was the most beautiful car they had ever seen. You wanted to know where your mommy got the car. Josie told you it was hers and that was all that mattered. You all spent time appreciating its beauty.

Josie said Gina had never been in a convertible before. Gina felt overwhelmed with excitement and begged Josie to take her for a ride. You were excited and wanted your mommy to take you for a ride, too. Josie told you and Gina she still had a few things to do and promised to take both of you for a ride later in the day. Josie asked Gina to take you for your favorite ice cream. You all went back inside, and Gina finished preparing lunch. Everyone sat down to eat, then Gina took you for ice cream at your favorite ice cream parlor.

Josie was home when Gina arrived back at the apartment. Within minutes, Josie and Gina began packing their suitcases. They locked up and went outside to the car. They placed the luggage in the trunk, and then Gina opened the passenger's door and helped you get into the backseat. Josie said you were all excited to go for a ride in the new car. The interior was beautiful. You sat in the center of the backseat, so Josie and Gina could keep an eye on you. You were having a great time.

"Mommy, I feel like a princess."

Just after they pulled away, the wind began blowing through your hair. You could hardly see.

"Gina, look! I'm flying."

Gina looked back. Josie could see you in her rearview mirror. You were moving your head from side to side. Waving your arms in the air.

"Where are we going, Mommy?"

You were always curious about everything.

"We are moving to Florida," said Josie.

"Daniella, you will like Florida," said Gina.

Your lives changed drastically that year. You, Josie, and Gina moved to North Florida that day. Josie and Gina took turns driving. It took all day and night, and you finally arrived the next afternoon.

"Where are we going to live?" you asked.

"We are going to visit my friends, the Johanssons, first. They are having a get-together today. I told them we would stop by and say hello."

For Josie it seemed like she drove forever. She had never been to the house before, so she wasn't quite sure how to get there. She hoped it wouldn't take long, because you were all tired.

Josie finally pulled up in front of a Colonial-style home. It was red brick and sat back away from the road. There were a lot of trees in the front yard. It had a long, curving driveway. There were four dormers on the second floor facing the street. There was a large screened front porch with a swing hanging from the ceiling.

Josie knew it was the right house. She could see children everywhere and could hear their laughter as she headed up the driveway to the house. When she stopped the car, everyone was eager to get out. It had been a long ride. You practically ran toward the back of the house where the kids were playing. Josie and Gina caught up with you. Mrs. Johansson walked up to introduce herself. Josie described her as very round and extremely pale. It didn't appear she had ever been out in the sun without a hat. She had black hair coiled up in a bun and wasn't wearing makeup. Josie had only spoken to her a couple of times. Josie and Gina both had a good feeling about her.

The Johanssons had adopted two boys, Tommy and Johnny. The boys were a year apart in age, about five or six years older than you. They didn't look anything alike. It was hard to believe they were brothers. Tommy was tall and had straight blond hair. Johnny was short and had curly brown hair. Josie said they had different fathers. Then there was Melissa. She was the Johanssons' daughter. Melissa was incredibly shy. She was a little chunky and had dark brown wavy hair and wore large black glasses. Melissa seemed withdrawn. You could tell she was trying to fit in. Melissa had little to say, but you seemed to like her a lot.

Usually, you were a bit shy with new people. On that day, you were on an emotional high. You couldn't stop talking. You were excited about the chance to play with the other kids. After Josie finished the introductions, you let go of Gina's hand and rushed over to where the other children were playing. Josie and Gina followed you, watching you interact with them. They enjoyed watching all the kids play. You seemed to be having fun and played for hours. Then the sun began to go down. No one wanted the day to end. People started leaving a few at a time.

When it was time to go, Gina called out for you. You were busy saying goodbye to your playmates. Gina walked over and took your hand, and both of you began walking toward the car where Josie was standing. When you arrived, Gina turned toward you and knelt. She gently placed a hand on each of your arms.

"Did you have fun today?" said Gina.

"Oh yes," you said enthusiastically.

Gina looked at Josie. She couldn't help but notice she got very quiet. She seemed to be miles away, deep in thought, and had a solemn look on her face.

You started to sense something was wrong.

"Gina? What's wrong? Why do you look so sad? Is something wrong?"

You were practically begging for a response.

"What's wrong, Gina? Is something wrong?"

You began to cry.

"Darling, something has come up. I wonder if you would mind staying with the Johanssons for a few days?"

Josie said you knew they were about to leave

you again.

"No, Gina! I don't want to stay with the Johanssons. I don't understand. I want to go home with you and Mommy."

Gina later told Josie it was heart-wrenching. She couldn't bear to see you so upset.

"You can't leave me here! Please don't leave me."

You began crying uncontrollably. Josie looked over. She could see the tears in Gina's eyes.

"Just for a few days, love. We'll come back to get you before you know it," she insisted.

Josie looked in the direction of the house. Gina's eyes followed hers. Mrs. Johansson was coming toward them. Josie walked to the back of the car and opened the trunk. You looked inside with curiosity. There were various totes and stacks of your clothing. You panicked when you saw them.

"I hate you! I hate you both!"

You were crying so hard they could hardly understand a word you were saying. You were more upset than they had ever seen you. Mrs. Johansson approached you. She placed her hand on your back and guided you toward the house.

"Come, dear," she said.

Mrs. Johansson looked over at Josie and Gina.

"She will adjust. I think it is a bit of a shock."

Mrs. Johansson had a very mild manner. She spoke in a sweet monotone voice.

"Please take good care of her," pleaded Gina.

Gina caught up with you. She leaned down and kissed you on the cheek.

"It will be okay, sweet girl. You'll see. We'll be back to get you before you know it."

Gina showed much more emotion than Josie did. By this time, Josie was numb. It was hard for her to feel much of anything.

"Come, dear. Let's go inside. Your mother told me you like chocolate milk," said Mrs. Johansson.

You and Mrs. Johansson continued to walk to the front door. You were crying feverishly. Josie and Gina got into the car and Gina slammed the door. Josie started the engine and began driving away. They never looked back. Josie would never forget how sad you and Gina were that day.

Josie called Mrs. Johansson later that night. Mrs. Johansson said she was nice to you. She did everything she could think of, but nothing seemed to make you feel any better. You didn't understand how they could leave you. She took you into the kitchen and poured you a glass of chocolate milk. She knew it was your favorite, but you refused to drink it. Mr. and Mrs. Johansson, Tommy, Johnny, and Melissa were there. You had just met them, and you were frightened.

A few hours later, Mrs. Johansson took you upstairs. She bathed you and helped you into your pajamas. Then she tucked you into bed. She sat in a chair next to you and tried to comfort you. She said you cried yourself to sleep.

Mrs. Johansson couldn't help but wonder how long it would take before you felt comfortable living in her home. It broke her heart to see you so sad. Some of the children adjusted quickly to their new surroundings. She worried you might be one of the ones that would not.

Josie called Mrs. Johansson again later that week. She told Josie you spent most of your time crying. You could not understand what was happening. You kept asking for Mommy and Gina and said you missed them. Mrs. Johansson continued to try to cheer you up. She said it wasn't easy. You were having temper tantrums. Mrs. Johansson said the hardest time was when you went to bed at night. For months, you cried yourself to sleep. Slowly, you began to fit into the Johansson family. Tommy and Johnny became your brothers and Melissa became your sister. Eventually, you got better, but you continued to have sad moments.

# Chapter Twelve

It was September 1955. You turned five in June. You had grown up faster than most children, and you understood much more than others your age. Josie was already beginning to feel the adverse effects her decision had taken on your lives.

Mrs. Johansson said there was a dramatic change in your behavior the day you climbed a tree in the backyard. You fell out and landed on your head. Head wounds bleed a lot and blood was everywhere. Mrs. Johansson rushed over to check your head. It turned out it was slightly worse than a small scrape. Then she checked your entire body.

You seemed to love the attention. You played it up and cried excessively, until you found out that Mrs. Johansson wanted to take you to the hospital. You stood and convinced her you were perfectly fine. Mrs. Johansson said she took you up to your room and bathed you and dressed you in your favorite pajamas. She gave you a loving hug and kissed you on the forehead. You both headed downstairs to the kitchen. Mrs. Johansson called out to the family:

"Dinner will be served in fifteen minutes."

Everyone rushed in and helped set the table. The family sat down and ate dinner. It was always a time when each of you shared your story of the day. You all finished dinner and cleaned up the kitchen.

Everyone gathered around the television to watch a movie. Mrs. Johansson wanted to keep an eye on you since you had hit your head earlier in the day. She snuggled with you on the sofa, under a soft, warm blanket. When the movie ended, Mrs. Johansson carried you upstairs to your bedroom and tucked you into bed. She slept in a chair alongside you. She wanted to continue to check on you periodically throughout the night.

You had been sad for quite some time. After you had fallen out of the tree, Mrs. Johansson said you relied on drama to get attention. You were always looking for reassurance that the family cared about you. You enjoyed having them fuss over you. They knew and went along with you. They constantly pampered you so they could show you how much they all loved you.

You spent your sixth birthday with the Johansson family. They filled the house with birthday decorations. They grilled hot dogs outside for all the kids in the neighborhood. Mrs. Johansson made a birthday cake for you. She wrote "Happy Birthday. We Love You, Daniella." You said it was the yummiest cake you had ever eaten. You got a lot of presents that day and you told everyone how much you loved them. You'd never had a birthday party before.

You started first grade that year. Mrs. Johansson took you to your first day of school. You liked being with all the other kids and they loved you. You did well in school.

Josie stayed in touch with Mrs. Johansson for a while. After she found out you were adjusting to your new life, she didn't call again for quite some time. When she finally did call, the conversation was brief. It was clear to Mrs. Johansson that Josie was at a loss for words. She asked, "How is Daniella doing? Is she getting along with the other children? Does she ever ask about us?" When Mrs. Johansson asked when your mother would be sending the money for your care, the conversation ended abruptly. It concerned Mrs. Johansson a great deal. She wasn't worried about the money. She was worried about Josie's lack of interest in her daughter.

***

My aunt Toni became very ill that winter and never quite recovered. Every time I called her, she tried to tell me more stories about my mother. I quickly realized that she could no longer recall many of the events of the past. I missed Toni's kindness and the chance to finally learn why my life was so different from the lives of the other kids I knew. Toni was the only connection I had to my family. I called from time to time to say hello. I think she remembered me, but I could never be sure. She passed away a few years later. Sadly, I never got the chance to say goodbye. I would have been lost if I had never contacted Toni. I believe her willingness to try to help me understand my past made a tremendous difference in the outcome of my future.

I tried to piece together Toni's last story with what I could remember. I recall the first time I saw my mother after she left me with the Johanssons.

# Chapter Thirteen

*I*t had been quite a while since I had seen my mother or Gina. Then one day, I was outside playing when I saw a big white Cadillac coming up the road. It looked like them. I couldn't believe it. It was her and Gina. The top was down and there was a man was sitting in the backseat. I didn't recognize him. He had dark, wavy hair and was wearing black sunglasses. My mother had a scarf around her head.

She came driving up like nothing had happened. She pulled into the driveway, throwing up dust and sand along the way. Gina was in the passenger's seat. She swung open the car door before the car came to a full stop and jumped out. Gina slammed the door shut and started running toward the area where I was playing. She was waving a large straw hat and had on a white dress and sandals. She was wearing a strand of pearls around her neck. She looked more beautiful than anyone I had ever seen. She looked like an angel.

"Baby, it's Gina!"

I could hear her yelling.

"Daniella!"

She kept waving her arms high above her head trying to get my attention.

"Daniella!"

She cut across the yard. There were rocks and tree stumps everywhere. She wasn't paying attention to where she was running. A couple of times, I thought she was going to fall. She would stumble and just keep coming. Gina was more excited than I had ever seen her. I started running toward her. I couldn't speak. I was exploding with excitement. She grabbed me and lifted me up. We went around and around, hugging and kissing.

"Gina!"

Tears of joy ran down my face. I never

remembered being so happy.

"I missed you so much. Where did you go? Why did you leave me?"

I never remembered feeling that way before. It was like floating through the air.

"It's a long story, baby. I know how terrible it must have been for you."

Gina always had a loving way about her. I believed everything she ever said to me.

"It couldn't hurt anyone more than it hurt me, baby. Trust me, I was heartbroken, but there was no other way."

By this time, my mother had gotten out of the car. She was walking toward us. She had on a flowered summer dress. I thought it looked nice on her. I didn't know what I thought about seeing her. There was a part of me that was happy and another part of me that was so angry with her that I couldn't look at her. The closer she got, the more anxious I became. Gina began putting me down until I could feel my feet touch the ground.

"Aren't you going to give your mother a hug?"

I stood there. I felt numb and I couldn't speak. My mother knelt and gently took my arms. She slowly pulled me toward her, but I pulled away.

I'm not sure what I was feeling, but she seemed to understand and didn't force it. I stepped back and kept looking at her. Both my mother and Gina were standing in front of me. I couldn't believe it.

The man in the car stayed in the backseat, watching from a distance. He looked over in our direction and smiled and nodded his head.

"Who is the man in the car?" I asked.

"He's a friend of mine, honey. I told him all about you. He wants to meet you," said my mother.

Before anyone could say anything more, Mrs. Johansson came out from inside the house. She was walking very fast toward us, and she didn't look happy. I could tell she was upset with my mother.

"You should have called. It would have been much better for you to have let us know that you were coming," insisted Mrs. Johansson.

"We are sorry. It was a spur of the moment thing. We were driving down the road and decided to come," my mother said apologetically.

Gina was trying hard to convince everyone to remain calm.

"I didn't know I needed an appointment to see my daughter." My mother had an angry look on her face.

"This is not the time to discuss this. We should talk about it later. We need to go inside. It's hot out here. We can visit on the porch for a while," Gina declared.

We began walking toward the house. My mother signaled her friend to come with us. He got out of the car and headed in our direction and met up with us. My mom introduced him to everyone as Dempsey. She said he was a friend. He shook everyone's hand and said hello. He nodded at me when my mother told him who I was. I thought he was shy.

We walked up to the porch. Mrs. Johansson always turned on the huge fans. It was a warm afternoon and they helped to cool us off. We visited for hours.

Mother and Gina took turns asking me questions about how I was doing. Some other kids came over and sat with us and talked. We shared some of our stories with them. I told them all about the presents I got for my birthday and the swing set I got for Christmas.

I asked them if they wanted to go up to see my room. My mother and Gina walked upstairs with me and Dempsey walked up behind us. I showed them my room and told them Mrs. Johansson painted it my favorite shade of blue. She let me help her decorate it. I liked it a lot. I rambled on about my life with the Johanssons and my friends who lived there with us. Dempsey sat and watched everything. He chuckled a few times, but never really said much. I wanted to ask my mother and Gina if they had come to get me, but I didn't. I was afraid of what they would say. Deep down, I already knew the answer.

It was getting late and the sun was starting to go down. We walked back downstairs, and everyone began saying their goodbyes. By then, there was no doubt in my mind they were leaving without me. I was sure my mother knew I had figured it out. Finally, she made it clear to me. She started making excuses and told me several times they would come back for me next weekend. After what she had done, I couldn't believe she would continue to tell me stories. I couldn't trust anything she said, and I knew she was lying to me. She must have thought I was young and stupid.

We walked them to their car, and they got in and left. I went back inside the house and cried for hours. Nothing could have made me feel better. They had deserted me again. The next weekend came and went and there was no sign of my mother or Gina. For weeks I thought about their next visit. There was a part of me that felt excited and the other part told me that there was a chance they weren't coming back. Like all the other times before, I was heartbroken.

# Chapter Fourteen

$\mathcal{M}$onths went by, and there was no sign of Mom or Gina. They never called to say they weren't coming. They just didn't show up. Their visit had proved to be unsettling. I began missing them all over again. It took me weeks to readjust to being with the Johanssons. I was sure I was not the only person in our house who wasn't happy they had come to visit. It was the first time I had ever seen Mrs. Johansson upset. Late one night, I overheard her and Mr. Johansson downstairs in the kitchen talking. They were speaking in a tone I hadn't heard before. I couldn't understand what they were saying, but I was sure it had something to do with my mother and Gina. Not long after, I could hear Mrs. Johansson on the telephone. I had a feeling she was talking to my mom. I stood at the foot of the stairs and tried to listen.

"You can't just walk in and out of her life whenever you choose. You are affecting her, so you need to make up your mind what you want to do. I am not happy with the way things are going. We love her. We all love her and she's happy here. Why don't you let us adopt her? We can give her a much better life. Do what's right for her. My husband and I have spoken to an attorney. All you need to do is sign the papers and she will become a Johansson."

There was a pause.

"You don't pay to take care of her, and you don't come to see her."

My mother must have said something that upset Mrs. Johansson even more. I peeked around the corner. I could tell by Mrs. Johansson's body language that she was angry. Her voice was escalating with every word. Mr. Johansson was trying to calm her down. He put his arm around her, but she pulled away. She stood and began shouting.

"Once! What's that? That's not a mother.

Just because you gave birth doesn't make you a mother!"

Mrs. Johansson had no idea I was lurking around the corner. She mumbled something, but I couldn't make it out. She got very upset and started crying.

"If we must declare you unfit, we will. We will not allow you to destroy Daniella's life."

Mrs. Johansson slammed down the phone. I peeked around the corner again. She pulled out a chair, covered her face with her hands, and wept. I felt sick. I didn't want her to know I had been listening. It broke my heart to see her so sad. Mr. Johansson pulled out a chair and sat next to her, trying to comfort her. He leaned over and placed his arm around her back and hugged her. I heard him tell her everything was going to work out.

A few minutes later they got up. I could see they were getting ready to walk out of the room. I didn't want them to see me, so I stood there for a moment. Then I crept back toward the steps and back up the stairs. I went to my room and lay on my bed.

There was a part of me that was angry with Mrs. Johansson for having said those terrible things to my mother. The other part of me understood why she had said them. The things she said were true. I wanted my mom to love me. There were times I thought I still loved her. My relationship with her had always been distant. Long before she left me, she'd always had her life and then there was me. I didn't fit in with the lifestyle she wanted to live. I wanted her to be like Mrs. Johansson. I wanted her to love me and want to be with me, but I never thought she did.

I always knew Gina loved me. She made me feel important in her life. Sometimes I felt upset with her. I didn't understand why she let my mother leave me with strangers. I convinced myself it wasn't up to her and that it was my mom's decision. I could never let myself believe it was Gina's fault.

I wanted to go home to be with my mother and Gina. I missed Gina much more than my mom. I also loved the Johanssons and wanted to stay with them. They were my family. I felt like crying, but the tears didn't come. I lay there for hours, staring at the ceiling. I was trying to understand why my life was different from the lives of the other kids I knew. Nothing made sense to me. I guess I was still too young.

Later, I heard Tommy and Johnny arguing about something. I got up and walked toward the door. I could hear them clearer now. Johnny accused Tommy of eating his socks.

"I can never find two that match!" Tommy said in a frustrated voice.

Sometimes Johnny and Tommy were ridiculous. They always made me laugh. I wished they could hear how they sounded. I chuckled and walked into the hall and confronted them.

"Eat your socks? Tommy didn't eat your socks; I did!"

We all looked at one another and began laughing hysterically.

"Seriously, I did! I ate your socks!"

I was sure Johnny and Tommy realized how silly they must have sounded. I charged toward the stairs and they both ran after me. I tackled each step with precision and was losing them, just before I tripped on the last step. Tommy and Johnny both pounced on top of me and began tickling me. I screamed with laughter at the top of my lungs. After a few minutes, we lay on the floor and laughed hysterically. We always had so much fun together. I could hear Mr. Johansson's footsteps coming around the corner.

"My goodness! What's happening in here? It's time to eat. Let's get up. We should go to the kitchen. Let's sit down and have a quiet meal," said Mr. Johansson.

The boys got up and straightened their clothes. They dusted off their shirts and pants. Mr. Johansson took my hand and helped me up.

"Kids, what shall we do with you?" he said.

I must have looked a mess. Mr. Johansson took one look at me, shook his head, and chuckled. We walked into the kitchen. We sat down at the table and got comfortable. Within minutes, the doorbell rang.

"I'll get it," said Johnny.

He was the closest to the door. He pushed back his chair, got up, and walked over. We could hear the door open and a strange commotion. There was a sound of scuffling. Mr. Johansson quickly jumped to his feet. I could hear Johnny in the other room call out to Mr. Johansson.

"Father!"

"What on earth is going on? Everyone stays here. I'll be right back," said Mr. Johansson.

We all jumped up to see what was happening.

Before Mr. Johansson reached the door, my mother, Gina, and Dempsey barged in. I couldn't believe it.

"What are you doing here?" I could tell Mrs. Johansson was angry.

"Daniella, get your sweater," demanded my mother.

"Why, Mother? Why do I need my sweater?"

I was shocked and confused.

"Get your sweater! Gina will go with you."

My mother's voice seemed to rise with each word. I could tell she was angry.

"Never mind!" said Mother. She took hers off and handed it to me.

"Put mine on."

"Gina, what's going on?"

I felt upset and begged for a response.

"Your mother told you to put on her sweater. Here, let me help you."

Gina began sticking my arms in the sleeves of my mother's sweater. It was big on me. Gina wrapped it around me.

"Let's go, now!" insisted Gina.

"I'm going to call the police," exclaimed Mrs. Johansson.

"Call them!" said my mother.

I could feel the tears trickle down my cheeks and I began to tremble.

"Children, go to your room," ordered Mr. Johansson.

He began shuffling the children toward the stairs.

"Go! Go upstairs."

Mother directed Gina and me to go to the car.

"Go! Now!" said my mother.

My mother and Gina both began leading me toward the front door.

"Go! Get in the car," my mother demanded.

"Mother, why are you doing this? Where are we going?"

There was too much confusion in the room. It was affecting me, and I started crying.

"Don't be afraid, honey. Everything is going to be all right. You'll see," said Gina.

My mother and Gina were both telling me not to worry. I had always trusted Gina. I knew she wouldn't lie to me. I was hesitant to trust my mom. I knew there were times when my mother lied to me. She also had a habit of leaving out important stuff.

Gina reached over and took my hand. We began rushing to the car. Dempsey jumped in front of Mr. and Mrs. Johansson, stopping them from getting close to me. Then Dempsey walked directly behind us.

"I'll be right there. Go!" insisted my mother.

My mother stayed behind for a few minutes. I could hear her and the Johanssons talking in a very upsetting tone. I couldn't make out what they were saying, but I was sure they were arguing. Gina continued to guide me toward the car. I was getting more upset by the minute.

"Gina, what's going on?"

I continued to cry.

Gina had a way of comforting me. She always made me feel protected. We stopped for a moment. She knelt and put her arms around me and hugged me.

"It's all right honey. Trust me, everything is going to be all right."

She spoke with kindness and compassion.

"Come on, baby. We need to go. I know it's confusing to you now, but it is going to be fine."

She stood, and we continued our rush to get to the car. Dempsey jumped ahead of us as he got closer to us. He opened the door and got into the backseat. Gina got into the passenger's side and pulled me onto her lap. She closed the door behind us.

"It's going to be me, you, and your mom again. We are all going to be together. It will be like old times. You would like that, wouldn't you, honey?"

She waited for my response.

"Yes, Gina! I always wanted to be with you. I thought you didn't want to be with me."

"We've decided you have stayed here long enough. We want you with us. Are you certain you want to be with us?"

"Yes, Gina! I want to be with you."

It still hadn't hit me I was leaving the Johanssons forever. It could have been the last time I would ever see them. At that very moment, all I could see was me, Mom, and Gina all together again.

My mother suddenly appeared and jumped into the car. She started the engine and began to drive away. I couldn't help but notice her looking in her rearview mirror. She was driving faster than I had ever remembered.

"Mother, why are you going so fast?" I asked.

"I'm sorry, dear. Am I going fast?"

She looked down at the speedometer.

"Well, I guess I should slow down a bit. Thank you for telling me, sweet girl. I didn't realize it."

Her glance at Gina was telling. She thought she needed to drive fast to get away from the Johanssons. I could tell my mother still didn't understand that I wasn't a baby anymore.

"Go!" shouted Dempsey.

My mom and Gina were quiet. Dempsey never said another word. I was exhausted. I wrapped my arms around Gina and held on to her tightly. I thought I was hugging an angel. I was happy, but the events of the day had exhausted me. Within minutes, I fell asleep peacefully.

# Chapter Fifteen

The next thing I knew, I woke up lying alongside Gina. I looked around the room. I was in a place I had never been before. I watched Gina sleep. Her hair and eyelashes were as dark as night and her skin was milky white. The contrast was extreme. She had a faint smile when she slept. I snuggled in closer, put my arms around her, and held her tightly. A while later she woke up and we hugged for a bit longer. She gave me a loving good morning kiss on the cheek. Soon after we got up and went into the kitchen, where my mother sat at the table drinking coffee.

"Coffee's fresh. I just made a pot."

Gina rubbed her eyes, still half asleep. She walked over and poured herself a cup. My mother went to the fridge and came back with a glass of milk. She set it down in front of me alongside a plate of my favorite peanut butter cookies. Then she reached down and put her arms around me.

"Good morning, Daniella. How's my girl? Did you sleep well?" she asked.

She tried to comfort me with her distant hug. Then she walked over and sat in a chair across from me.

"Yes, Mother."

There I was with Gina and my mother. We were all together again. I couldn't believe it. My mother and Gina talked about their plans for the day. My mom had to work for a few hours, so Gina and I decided to go shopping to buy me some clothes. I was excited to have a chance to spend the day shopping with my favorite person. I couldn't have been happier. I felt as if I were walking on clouds as I danced around the room.

After my mother left for work, Gina and I headed to the mall. Once we arrived and parked, we began walking in and out of every store. We were having fun together. I must have tried on fifty outfits. Gina said I looked cute in all of them. I think she got a little carried away. I didn't like the outfit with the bows all over it. Fortunately, we didn't get that one. She bought me a lot of clothes. She said she thought I would outgrow most of them before I got a chance to wear them.

Afterward, we went to a great pizza place. We could hardly move we ate so much. We complained that we felt stuffed. I was tired and ready to go home. Gina still wanted to shop, but I finally convinced her I couldn't take another step. Soon after we got home, we began unloading the car. I saw my mom's car outside. She was home from work. She stopped Gina when we got to the front door.

"Go to your room, Daniella. I need to speak to Gina for a minute," she insisted.

Now what? I knew that look. I did as my mother said. I took the packages to my room and began tearing into every bag. I opened them and laid my new clothes on the bed. Standing in front of the floor mirror, I displayed each outfit against my body and imagined what they would look like with my new shoes and socks. Not long after, Gina came into the room. She walked over to me and knelt. I was right.

"Honey, how would you like to go to Miami? You have always wanted to go to Miami, right?"

Gina had a serious look on her face. Somehow, I knew the only answer was yes. I knew we were going to Miami. I just didn't know why. Sure enough, before I got a chance to find out, my mother came into the room. She threw a suitcase on the bed and Gina began tossing my clothes inside.

"Let's hurry. I want to get on the road before it gets dark," insisted my mother.

Gina and I stared at each other for a moment. A couple of minutes later, I began helping her pack. My mom kept coming in and out of the room, pressuring us to rush. We finished and headed out the front door. Gina and Mother threw our luggage in the trunk and we jumped into the car. Within a few minutes, we were pulling out of the driveway. I sat in the backseat and got comfortable. I couldn't believe it. Just like that, we were on our way to Miami. I was more confused than usual. At that point, everything seemed strange to me. I was afraid to ask why we were going to Miami. There was one thing for certain. There was never a dull moment with these two.

We were in the car for a long time. My mother

and Gina took turns driving. One rested while the other drove. Gina told me we weren't stopping until we got where we were going. We got gas a couple of times and used the bathroom. We picked up a few bags of my favorite chips and soda and got back in the car and continued our drive. My mother told me when we crossed into Miami that we were heading to Miami Beach. There weren't any clouds in the sky, and it was hot. The trees and grass were green, and there were a lot of flowers everywhere.

We finally arrived in Miami Beach. We drove around and looked at everything and went up and down a street close to the ocean. My mother said it was Collins Avenue. There were huge hotels and beautiful buildings everywhere. I had never seen anything like it. My favorite was when we were coming up to this one hotel that had a picture painted on the side of the wall. I loved that one. There were people and cars all over the place. We finally stopped and pulled in front of one of the hotels. The second we arrived, my mother jumped out of the car and headed inside the lobby.

"Wait here," she said.

Within minutes, several young men surrounded our car. They were there to help us get our luggage inside. We didn't stop at the desk or check in. We got on the elevator and headed to our room.

Immediately after we got there, we began to unpack. The room was nicer than any place we had ever lived or stayed. There were two king-size beds. There was a large sofa and a television in the corner. There was a small kitchen with all kinds of my favorite food in the cabinets and fridge. We liked our new place. We had never stayed anywhere so beautiful. Gina and I danced around the room with joy. After we checked everything out, we lay on the bed. Soon after, we were sleeping. The trip had tired us out. We slept for hours until the phone rang.

The manager of the hotel called my mother and invited us to go up to his room to visit him. We began waking up and deciding what we each wanted to wear. My mother and Gina took turns taking a shower. Then Gina bathed and dressed me. Once we finished, my mother inspected us to make sure we looked our best. We locked up and headed upstairs to meet with the manager of the hotel.

When he opened the door, we stood there, speechless. It wasn't a room. It was almost the entire top floor of the hotel. It was incredible. He had signed pictures of movie stars on his walls. There were fancy lights and nice stuff everywhere. I couldn't get enough. I wanted to walk around and look at everything, but my mother stopped me. I couldn't help but wonder what we were doing there. My mom introduced me to a large man she called Big Al. He asked us to sit and spoke in a deep and intimidating voice. We sat close to one another. He told my mother she had a beautiful daughter. I blushed and thanked him.

I couldn't imagine how my mother and Gina knew this big man. They seemed to enjoy being around him. He had a wonderful sense of humor. He talked for a while about the hotel. Then he got up and showed us around his apartment. I could have spent hours walking around and looking at everything. I couldn't believe how beautiful some of the paintings were. He told us they were all originals autographed by the artists. He had signed footballs, baseballs, tennis rackets, and all kinds of other stuff. I could tell he enjoyed telling me how he got each one. I didn't mind. I shared his enthusiasm. I had never seen anything like it before. I liked Big Al. He had lots of great stories to tell. I wanted to hear more, but my mother and Gina were ready to leave.

A short time later, they walked me back down to our room. Gina told me a woman named Gladys would be staying with me for a while. Gladys was waiting for us when we got there, and Mother introduced us to each other. Gladys seemed nice. We watched television together until I fell asleep on the sofa. My mother and Gina came back hours later. I didn't quite wake up, but I was aware of Gina picking me up and putting me to bed. She always leaned in and kissed me good night on the forehead.

When I woke up the next morning, I admired my surroundings. Although I was still curious, it didn't care enough to ask. I was there with my mother and Gina, and we were together again. I knew I could never be happier than I was when I was with them. We got dressed and headed downstairs to the dining room. The hostess sat us at a table for eight people. Not long after were seated, Big Al and four other guys came and sat with us. Their nicknames were Lucky, Lefty, Louie, and Tony. He referred to them as "the boys." Big Al said he and the others wanted to show us the other restaurants and clothing stores in the area. The three of us smiled with sincere enthusiasm.

After we finished eating, Big Al paid the bill.

Then we headed out for a tour of the town. We went in and out of most stores. Every time we saw something we liked, they bought it for us. They spent the day showing us fancy restaurants and promised to take us out to dinner at each one.

On that day, Big Al and the boys became part of our family. I loved being there with them. I liked Big Al best of all. He was a big teddy bear. He had a huge smile. He loved explaining and teaching me things. I don't know when he first stole my heart, but I remember him today as though my time with him was yesterday. The boys were funny. I laughed a lot when I was with them. Everyone was always smiling, laughing, and joking. It was one of the happiest times of my life.

One day my mother came into our room and told us it was time for us to leave. Leaving people behind was the only thing consistent in my life. It didn't take long for me to realize I might never see Big Al and the boys again. I couldn't stop crying. I was heartbroken. Big Al and the boys had made a lifelong impression on me that summer. Big Al had touched my heart in a way no one else had before him. We spoke on the telephone often after we left Miami, but I missed Big Al's giant hugs every day of my young life.

I wouldn't learn the significance of Big Al and the boys or the Miami Beach hotel for more than forty years.

# Chapter Sixteen

*W*ithin a couple of days, we were packed and starting our journey to the next destination. When I got into the car, Gina told me we were headed back to North Florida. Honestly, I didn't care where we were going. The only thing that mattered was that we were leaving our friends. We didn't say much to each other on the way north. I curled up in the backseat and cried myself to sleep. Other than a few restroom breaks, the trip was uneventful. I didn't care much about what was going on around me. I wasn't ready to be excited about anything or anybody. I was not happy about leaving Big Al and the boys.

Finally, we arrived at a large downtown area. It was late at night and there were cars lined up and down the street. There were a lot of hotels, theaters, and stores, and the streets were full of people. We parked in front of one of the hotels, a tall plain red brick building. The minute we arrived; my mother jumped out of the car the same way she had when we arrived at the Miami Beach hotel. Within minutes, several young men came out. They started unloading the car, and we walked inside. There was a sign on the column by the door: *Built in 1925*. The lobby of the hotel was even nicer than the hotel we had stayed at in Miami Beach. We walked over to the elevators, and within a few minutes we were on our way to our room.

We arrived and opened the door. I couldn't help but notice the room was smaller than the one we had before. It was nice, but it wasn't as nice as the one in Miami Beach. As always, we unpacked.

A few minutes later, there was a knock at the door. My mother opened it, and there was a woman was standing there. She introduced herself as Ruthie. She told us she was there to stay with me while my mother and Gina went out. Like the times before, I stayed behind. She helped bathe me and put me to bed. It had been a long day and I was tired. I missed Big Al and the boys. I told Ruthie all about them and how much I missed them. I was sad, and she tried to comfort me but couldn't. I cried myself to sleep.

Within a few days, I met my mother and Gina's new friends. Their names were Sammy, Louie, and Frankie. They were nice to me. I could tell they were trying to cheer me up, but I didn't want to like them too much. I knew we would leave again like all the times before.

We stayed at the hotel for a while. School started, and everyone took turns taking me and picking me up each day. I spent more time with the guys than I did with my mother and Gina. As expected, my mother came home one day and told us to start packing. At that point, I didn't care anymore. It was what we always did. We packed. I didn't bother to ask where we were going. I just got into the car, crawled into the backseat, and waited to arrive at our next place. We drove for a while and eventually pulled up in front of a large old house with a huge front yard. There were lots of children everywhere. Suddenly, I felt ill. I asked with the same curiosity I always did.

"Mother, who lives here? Gina, who are these people?"

Within a few moments, I knew they were getting ready to leave me again. I burst into tears. My mother stopped the car and opened her door. Then she reached into the backseat and pulled me out of the car.

"You are leaving me here, aren't you? I hate you! I hate you both!"

I was angry. I didn't want to see Gina or my mother. I never said goodbye to either of them. I turned and rushed toward the house. A large tall woman walked up to me and took my hand. She led me to the front door. I yelled out at the top of my lungs: "Go away! Don't come back! Ever! I hate you both!"

I felt more upset than I had ever been. I walked through a screened porch area and into the house. I watched out of a window as my mother and Gina removed my bags from the car. I couldn't believe this was happening again. I could see my mother and Gina speaking to one of the women outside. Gina was crying, but I didn't care. At that moment, I hated her and my mother. I saw them walk over and get into the car. I left the window before they drove away.

The lady who walked me into the house said her name was Mrs. Anderson. She took me upstairs, helped me with my bath, and dressed me in my pajamas. Then she tucked me into bed. I didn't say a word to her the entire time. She was trying to comfort me, but I wanted nothing to do with her or anyone else.

I stayed in bed for days and cried endlessly. I cried so hard, I made myself sick. One of the young girls came into the room and told me her name was Stacey. She tried to cheer me up, but I had nothing to say to her. Once again, I fell asleep from exhaustion.

I thought Mom, Gina, and I were a family. I believed we were happy together. I never thought they would leave me again. Like so many times before, they dropped me off at a stranger's house. I tried to figure out what I had done that made them so upset with me. Was it something I had said? I thought they loved me. I felt more confused, desperate, and lonely than I had ever been. I missed Gina, Big Al, and the boys. I wondered if I would ever see any of them again.

Now I was living with the Andersons. There were people everywhere, but I didn't know anyone. It was worse than the other times. I didn't even know their names.

Almost immediately, the Andersons began including me in everything. I could tell they were trying to comfort me. They wanted to make me feel like part of their family. Everyone was nice, but I didn't care. I couldn't understand why my mother and Gina were constantly leaving me with strangers. Every time I turned around, I was living with more people I didn't know. My mother and Gina had abandoned me again. I was having an awful time getting over it. I was frustrated and I cried and screamed a lot. I felt angry and hurt.

No one ever spoke of my mother or Gina. No one ever asked me about them. I couldn't imagine why. I always thought it was weird. Why didn't someone say something? *What does your mom do? When is she coming to get you? Are you related to Gina?* No one ever asked me anything about them, and it bothered me a lot. I wanted to talk to someone about my family. I prayed someone would ask me about them because I couldn't bring it up myself. I didn't think anyone cared about what I thought, or what I had to say. So, I just kept it all inside. I was too miserable to bother trying to fit in anymore.

Just like all the other times, I finally adjusted to my new home. Stacey was the Andersons' daughter. She and I became good friends. We were close in age. She played the piano, and I loved listening to her play. We hung out together most of the time. The school we attended was close to our house. We walked to school together every day.

She told me about each of the children who stayed at the home. Most of them stayed there during the day when their mothers worked. They paid the Andersons hourly to have them care for their child. Some of the kids lived with them all the time. Our parents agreed to pay them money to help with our care. I knew my mother wasn't going to pay them. I wondered if they would let me stay. I didn't want to have to move again.

Every Sunday, there was a huge picnic outside. If the weather wasn't great, the picnic was inside on the screened porch. Our parents could visit us on Sundays, but they had to leave when it started to get dark outside.

Every week most of the children's parents

came, but I just sat on the porch and looked outside. I waited for Gina and my mom, but they never came. Months went by, but they didn't call or write. No one heard from them. I eventually figured out they weren't coming back. I cried a lot because it angered me much more than it hurt me. Stacey and the Andersons tried to make me feel loved. We didn't speak about the fact that my mother and Gina didn't call, write, visit, or send money. I am certain they knew it would upset me.

One day they asked me to go into the study. That's what they called the room with all the books in it. It was where the parents met with the Andersons when they wanted to talk without the kids around. Stacey went with me and we sat and waited for them to come in. Mrs. Anderson sat down in front of me. She had a sad look on her face.

"Daniella, we have tried desperately to reach either your mother or Gina. It seems they disappeared from the face of the earth. We can't continue to ignore reality. The truth is, we don't know if they are coming back. At this point, we have lost hope."

She spoke every word slowly. I knew she was trying not to hurt my feelings. Most things that involved my mother and Gina were painful

"You know we love you like a daughter. We wanted to know how you feel. We would feel blessed if you would allow us to file for adoption. We want you to have a family you can call your own. We don't want to continue to see you suffer when you don't hear from your mother or Gina."

She looked straight into my eyes. I knew she felt my pain. I burst into tears. I was heartbroken about my mother and Gina, but I was happy to know the Andersons loved me. We all hugged, cried together, and eventually smiled together.

"Yes, I would love to be your daughter. I am tired of moving around. I don't want to see them ever again. If they loved me, they wouldn't keep leaving me."

We all got up and hugged one another. Stacey was excited and wanted me to know how happy she would be to have me as her sister. Mrs. Anderson told me I could always live there with them. I would never have to move again.

The next day the Andersons contacted an attorney. Mrs. Anderson told me everything as it was happening. She said they had filed for my adoption. The attorney told them it wouldn't be easy. The fact that my mother had left me there might be helpful. She had not come to see me in more than a year. Mrs. Anderson said they had a written agreement. My mom agreed to pay money every month and she never paid them. The Andersons told me they filed for adoption on the grounds that she was unfit and had abandoned me. I knew my mother wasn't a fit mother. A fit mother doesn't desert their kid. It was hard for me to hear, but I was getting older and I was beginning to understand. I was tired of moving and never wanted to move again.

The Andersons hired a private investigator named David to find my mother. Many months went by. Finally, David found her. He told the Andersons my mother had moved around a lot. She was living in a bad part of town. It seemed to him she might have been hiding from someone. My mother told him she didn't have a job. David said he could tell she was tired and worn out. He said he could find no sign of Gina. When David asked my mother about her, my mom said one day Gina packed up and left and she had no idea where she had gone. She said she never heard from her again.

David told my mother the Andersons had filed for adoption. He said she just sat there. She didn't say much. She just listened. David thought he should give her a chance to process the information. He said my mother was devoid of any emotion. Nothing anyone told me about her surprised me, especially the part where she was devoid of any emotion. I felt upset that Gina wasn't with her. I worried that David couldn't find her and wondered whether something might have happened to her. Gina never spoke to us about her family. I don't think she had anywhere else to go. I think we were her only family. She loved my mother and me. I knew Gina wouldn't just pack and leave without saying goodbye. That part did not make sense to me.

# Chapter Seventeen

Then one day unexpectedly, Mrs. Anderson received a letter in the mail. My mother had hired a lawyer, Lacy Masters. I overheard Mr. Anderson say he was one of the most expensive lawyers in the area. They wondered how she could afford to hire him. In the letter, he asked if the Andersons would meet with him and my mother in his office. They were shocked! My mom was always unpredictable. Nothing she did ever made sense to me. I wondered why she had hired a lawyer to fight the adoption. Until recently, no one had said she couldn't have me. If she wanted me so badly, why didn't she come to get me? Now she couldn't have me, so now she hired a lawyer to fight to keep me. It was confusing.

The Andersons agreed to meet with Mr. Masters and my mother. Mr. Masters encouraged the Andersons to have their attorney present. He didn't think I should be there. They scheduled the meeting for the following week. Reluctantly, the Andersons went to meet with them at Mr. Masters's office.

When they returned from the meeting, the Andersons told me my mother would have scheduled visitation rights. Both attorneys agreed the visits would continue until they settled the case. I made it clear to everyone I wasn't happy about having to spend time with her.

Mrs. Anderson told me we needed to meet with my mother later that day. She drove us to a little café close to the house. As we walked inside, I could see my mom sitting at a table across the room. I hardly recognized her when she stood up. She didn't look like herself. Her hair was blond, she was overly tanned, and her skin had a leathery appearance. She was very skinny, and she wore an outfit that didn't look attractive on her. I was young, but I was old enough to know something was going on with her. We all sat at a table in the back of the restaurant. My mother sat directly across from me.

"Hello, Daniella. How is my sweet girl today?"

I wasn't interested in having any contact with her. Gina wasn't there.

"Where is Gina?"

"She is gone."

"Gone where?" I asked.

"I have no idea where she went. I came home one day, and I discovered she had moved out."

"Why did she move out? Why didn't she tell you where she was going?"

My mother didn't respond. Somehow, I knew there was more to the story.

I was angry with Gina, but I never imagined I would never see her again. I was heartbroken, and it didn't seem right she wasn't there. We ordered lunch, but I could barely eat. My mom was asking me a bunch of stupid questions. I gave short answers. I wasn't in the mood to speak to her.

We stayed just over an hour. Finally, we stood and said our goodbyes. Once again, my mother tried to reach out to me. I turned my back and walked toward the door. She was nobody to me. At that moment, I had no feelings for her. On the ride home, no one said a word. I sat back in my seat and stared out the window.

Weeks went by and she never even called to say hello. It didn't matter to me. She had never behaved like a mother. Then out of the blue, Mrs. Anderson came into my room one day. She had a strange look on her face.

"Daniella, I need to get you dressed. Your mother will be here to pick you up shortly. You will be spending a couple of days with her."

I made it clear to Mrs. Anderson I wasn't happy about going anywhere with my mother. When she finished dressing me, we went downstairs. A few minutes later, there was a knock at the door. I knew it was my mother. Mrs. Anderson opened it and there she stood.

"Hello, Daniella! How is my sweet girl? I came to take you for a ride in my new Cadillac."

Mrs. Anderson handed my mother an overnight bag with a few of my clothes in it.

"Goodbye, Daniella. I will see you late Sunday. Have a lovely time with your mother."

It had been a couple of months since I had seen my mother at the café. I stood for a moment and tried to understand why I had to go with her. Then I walked outside, headed slowly toward her car, and she followed behind me. She walked over to the passenger's side, opened the door for me, and helped me get in. I looked back, and I could see Mrs. Anderson waving goodbye. Then my mother went around to the other side of the car, got in, and started the car. While we were in the car, she tried to talk to me, but I didn't have much to say.

We ended up in a neighborhood with little houses that all looked alike. The only thing different was the colors. We pulled into the driveway of one of them and got out of the car. A young boy walked over. That was the first time I met Billy.

"Are you guys moving here?" he asked.

I couldn't help but notice the blue color of his eyes. I thought they were beautiful.

"Yes," said my mother.

The boy responded, "If you need anything, you should tell my mom. She lives here with me."

He pointed to the house next door.

"My mom calls me Billy. What's your name?"

"Daniella."

"Can you come over? I want you to meet my mom."

He was very excited, but my mother made it clear it wasn't the right time. We walked up to the front door of the house and went inside. The interior of the house looked freshly painted. I could smell the paint. Everything was spotless and the furniture appeared to be new. I thought it was a model home. It didn't look like anyone had ever lived there.

"Come on. I will show you around," said my mother.

I went in and out of every room. To my surprise, my mom had one of the rooms painted my favorite shade of blue.

"This will be your room when you come to visit. Do you like it? I tried to get as close to the blue as you had when you lived at the Johanssons'," said Mother.

"It's nice. Do you live here?" I asked.

"Yes, I bought this house for us," she said.

I wasn't paying attention to anything she was saying to me. I liked the room, but I wasn't going to tell her. My mom laid my bag on the bed, opened it, and started taking out my clothes. She put them away in the dresser drawers. I sat on the bed and watched her, but we didn't say a word to each other.

"Can I go outside and play with Billy?" I

asked.

"Don't you want to see the rest of the house?" asked my mother.

"Sure. Can we do it later?" I asked.

"I guess we can," said my mother.

She looked disappointed, but I didn't care. I practically ran outside. I went next door to Billy's house and knocked on his door. He seemed excited to see me. Billy made me feel welcome. He introduced me to his mother, Jennifer. She was nice. Then Billy took me to his backyard, where he had a playhouse. We hung out most of the afternoon. That was the day Billy and I became friends. Billy seemed happy, and I hoped some of his happiness would rub off on me. Whenever I visited my mother's house, I headed straight to see Billy. We spent most of our free time together.

My mom always had a lot of friends hanging around. People were constantly coming and going. It took a while, but I was finally happy when I was there. The relationship between my mother and me didn't change much. She was still ice-cold. I almost felt sorry for her. I could tell she was trying to take care of me, but she had no idea what to do.

The kids in the neighborhood nicknamed her

"the ice princess." I understood, but it hurt my feelings. She never showed emotion. She rarely hugged me, and when she did it was weird.

Sometimes my mother would tuck me in at night. She wouldn't say much. She fluffed my pillow, pulled the blanket over me, kissed me on the forehead, and said good night. Then she would turn out the light and leave the room.

One day a guy came over to the house. She called him Jason. He was very handsome. He wasn't very tall, and he had big shoulders. Jason had medium-colored skin, dark hair, and the bluest eyes I had ever seen. I liked blue eyes. I couldn't help but stare back at them when he looked at me. Jason started coming over every day. He was generous with his time and emotions. Jason played with me. We had fun. He often took my mother and me out to eat. Sometimes he took us to the movies and playgrounds. He took us anywhere we wanted to go. Occasionally, Billy would go with us.

I guess you could say Jason was my mother's boyfriend. It was noticeable that he liked her. I could never tell how she felt about him. My mother was as cold to Jason as she was with me. The more I saw of him, the closer I got. He was hard not to love. He was sweet and he showed me every day how much I meant to him. I grew to love Jason like no one else I had ever known. As time went on, my world revolved around him. I thought he lived for the sole purpose of trying to make me happy.

I still missed Gina and Big Al. Gina was the first person I'd ever loved. I thought about her every day. Before Jason, Big Al had been the father figure in my life. He gave the best bear hugs ever. I would always miss Gina, Big Al, and the boys, but my new life was getting better.

# Chapter Eighteen

Christmas was incredible that year. Billy's mom bought him a cute little gray and white puppy. We named him Smokey. We couldn't wait to come home from school every day so we could play with him. I was captivated by everything Smokey did. I would get upset at night when he went home with Billy. We would fight over him, but I always lost. After all, he was Billy's dog.

I am sure my mom could see how much I liked playing with the puppy. One day she asked me if I wanted one. The next time I went to her house, she had bought me the cutest German Shepherd

Husky mix. We named him Champ. Champ and Smokey got along great. Billy and I would hang out and watch them play together for hours. Nothing brought me more happiness than Champ, Smokey, and Billy.

Every week I went back and forth from the Andersons' house to my mother's house. It was a confusing way to live. I looked forward to the day I wouldn't have to do it anymore. Months went by. The adoption proceedings seemed to be taking forever. They had turned into a war. I tried to ignore everything around me as much as I could.

Jason was always at my mom's house when I was there. One day my mother asked me if I could sit with them and talk for a while. Sitting and talking with my mother always made me nervous. I wasn't ready for any more of her surprises.

"It's okay, Daniella. There's nothing wrong. I wanted to talk to you about Jason and me. We have been thinking about getting married. We wanted to know how you would feel about it. What you think is important to us. If I marry him, that will make him your stepfather."

I was speechless. I loved Jason. He was amazing.

"If I marry him, we could all live here as a family. You wouldn't have to continue to go back and forth between the Andersons and us."

I thought about it for a minute. It was a big decision. I knew if I said yes, I would never see the Andersons again.

"You could see Champ every day if you lived here. If you end up living with the Andersons, Champ will need to stay here with us. You know Mrs. Anderson doesn't allow animals in her home."

Then she said the magic words.

"If you don't live here, we may not be able to keep Champ. We work too many hours. I don't know how we would be able to care for him. We couldn't leave him at home by himself all day. That wouldn't be fair to him.

"You don't need to decide right this minute. Think about it and let us know. Your happiness is the most important thing to us. We would like it if you gave us your approval."

I am sure they could see the excitement on my face. I was deliriously happy with the idea of having Jason as a stepfather. He had always been wonderful to me. I loved the thought of being able to play with Champ and Smokey every day. Billy was my best friend and he lived next door. I needed to think.

"I need for you to promise not to ever mention our private conversation about Jason and Champ to anyone. It must be our little secret. Promise me, sweet girl?"

"I promise, Mommy."

It was a difficult time for me. Every time I went home to be with my mother, Champ, and Jason, I missed the Andersons. Every time I went to see the Andersons, I missed Champ and Jason. I would like to say I missed my mom, but I still had bad feelings about her. I blamed her for Gina leaving us, and I never forgave her for losing contact with her. I was angry with her for leaving me with people I didn't know, and I hated her for not coming back when she said she would. I was annoyed that we never had time to visit Big Al and the boys. It was going to take more than a house, a puppy, and Jason to make me forgive my mother for all she had done. I wasn't sure I ever could.

The next time I went to see my mother, she and Jason had gotten married. I couldn't hide the fact that I was happy about it. We all danced around the room. I played with Jason and Champ. My mom even played with us for a while.

Then Jason knelt, leaned in, and kissed me on the cheek. He reached out and gently placed his hands over mine. Jason looked at me like I was his little angel. I could see the love on his face.

"Daniella, would you like to call me Daddy? I would be honored to be your father."

I felt overwhelmed with joy and could feel tears rolling down my cheeks. He hugged me the way Big Al used to hug me.

"Yes, Daddy! Yes!"

We shared a beautiful moment. Jason became my stepfather that day.

A month or so later, the judge ordered a closed meeting in his chambers. He asked the Andersons to make sure I was present. The Andersons discussed it with me. They wanted me to know what to expect. Mrs. Anderson made me promise to be honest, no matter what questions the judge asked me.

I doubted anything I said or wanted would matter. I was too young to make decisions. However, I met with the judge, the Andersons, the attorneys, my mother, and Jason. The judge started to ask me questions about my life.

"Hello, Daniella. Thank you for coming to see me today. I thought we could just sit and talk. I wanted to find out how you are doing. I know you have been living in two different homes for a while now. I am sure it's been difficult for you. Tell me about your visits with the Andersons."

I had no problem sharing my feelings.

"I love the Andersons. I know they love me, too. They treat me like I'm their kid. Their daughter, Stacey, and I are close in age. She is like a sister to me."

I am sure they could see the love I felt toward the Andersons.

"How about your mother and Jason? I understand your mother married Jason. What do you think about having him as a stepfather?"

I remembered what my mom said about Champ. She told me that if I didn't live with her, she would have to give him away. I couldn't let that happen. I had promised her I wouldn't tell a soul about our private conversation. I had to be convincing.

"It's been good. It's taken a while for me to feel okay with my mother. It's gotten much better. I have a new friend named Billy. He lives next door. He has a dog named Smokey and I have a dog named Champ. We like to watch them play together." I took a deep breath and continued my story.

"I love Jason. Jason asked me if I wanted to call him Daddy. I told him I did. We have a nice house and I have my own bedroom. They painted it my favorite color of blue. My mom is working as a waitress. She comes home after work and cooks us dinner. We all watch television together at night. Then she bathes me and puts me to bed. She and Jason always come to my room before I go to sleep. They both kiss me on the forehead and tell me they love me. Then they turn out the lights."

I sang like a bird. I knew I had one chance to keep Champ, so I needed to be convincing. Eventually, we all got up and said our goodbyes. I went home with the Andersons that day.

Months passed without a word. Then the Andersons' attorney let us know the judge had made his final decision. We met back in the judge's chambers. That's when the judge told us his decision. He had granted my mom and Jason full custody of me. Mrs. Anderson broke down into tears and Mr. Anderson tried to comfort her. I ran over and grabbed her. We hugged one another and cried together. It was heartbreaking to see her sad. I had given up the hope of having a real family of my own until the Andersons had come along. I felt terrible. It hurt me to know that I was the cause of Mrs. Anderson's pain. I knew there was nothing I could do to make her feel better. I had a feeling it would be like everyone else who had ever come into my life. I would never see the Andersons again, but living in two places was unsettling. I was glad it was finally over, but it didn't make it any less painful.

After everyone calmed down, we said goodbye. I left with my mother and Jason that day. Within a few weeks, the Andersons packed up my clothes and toys and delivered everything that belonged to me to my mother's house. I got to see the Andersons one last time.

I was eight years old when the judge made his final decision. When I looked back years later, I realized my mother had manipulated me. She wanted me to tell the judge how much I loved mommy and daddy. I wasn't certain my conversation with the judge was the reason it turned out the way it did, but I realized the importance of my meeting with him and had no doubt it was instrumental in his final decision.

The Andersons spent a lot of money trying to adopt me. I felt bad for them, but their attorney was no match for Lacy Masters. They didn't have a chance. He was worth every penny my mother paid him. He had devised a well-orchestrated plan.

The events of that year were bittersweet. I wondered if there would ever be an end to the chaotic life I was living. My life was changing again. How many more times would I have to move before I had a real home of my own?

# Chapter
## Nineteen

A couple of years later, one of my mother's brothers found us in North Florida. He called to tell my mother that their parents wanted to see us. They came for a visit that summer and stayed with us for a few months. My mom finally reunited with her family. I met my grandparents for the first time, and they met me. It was wonderful.

After their visit, we attended the annual family reunions. It was something to look forward to every year. More than sixty family members were always in attendance. My mother spent time getting reacquainted with her favorite sister, Toni. They spent countless hours catching up on stories of events that had happened during their years apart. No one ever mentioned the day their father had thrown my mom out of the house. It seemed time had healed a lot of wounds. We all stayed close until the deaths of my grandparents. After they died, there were no more family reunions.

During the next few years, I continued to do well in school. I enjoyed being around other kids every day. It reminded me of the times I spent with the Johanssons and the Andersons. I often wondered what my life would have been like had I continued to live with one of them.

For a while, life was mostly uneventful. Then one night shortly after my mom and dad came home from work, they got into a huge fight. I had never seen them so angry with one another. They sent me to Billy's house. We could hear yelling and screaming coming from my parents' home. It was concerning.

Eventually, my parents came and got me. I noticed my mother had a bandage on her nose. I couldn't imagine my father would ever hit her. They both looked visibly shaken. We didn't speak about anything that night. They told me to go to my room.

I woke up the next morning and walked into the living room. I could see a sign in our front yard from the window. I opened the door to take a closer look. It was a "For Sale" sign. I asked my parents why we were moving.

My dad responded, "Don't worry about it. We will get a bigger and better house."

My mother responded, "Why does it matter? We are moving, and that's all you need to know!"

I called Billy to find out whether his mom knew anything. She said she didn't. We were very close to our neighbors. Everyone knew one another. I called around that day, but no one seemed to know anything. I saw several of our neighbors. They didn't admit to me that they knew about the incident. No one even asked why our house had a For Sale sign in our yard. It was a mystery to me. Like a lot of things in my life, I would not learn the significance of these events until I was much older.

Billy and I were devastated. We couldn't believe my parents and I were moving. Unfortunately, our house sold more quickly than expected, so my parents rented an apartment on the beach. Billy and I continued to see each other, but it wasn't the same as walking next door after school and playing in the backyard whenever we wanted. Arrangements had to be made. One of our parents had to drop us off and pick us up. We rarely had time to let Champ and Smokey get together so they could play.

We lived at the beach for about a year. Then we moved into a beautiful ranch-style home. It was twice the size of our first home. Each house in the neighborhood had character. There was a huge five-bedroom next door and a small two-bedroom across the street. My mom had the house decorated by an interior decorator. It had style, charm, and the best of everything. It was a great house.

After we moved into the new house, some things changed. Before, my mother would go out at night without my father. Now, they always went out together. My mother dyed her hair back to brown. She always dressed in the best clothes that money could buy. She flaunted expensive jewelry everywhere she went. She also had several beautiful mink coats and never left the house in the winter without wearing one of them.

I had always resented my mother for taking me away from the Andersons. I couldn't understand why she had fought so hard to keep me. I rarely saw her or Jason. She never took part in any of my school functions. She was my mother, but she didn't act like a mother. Our relationship continued to be distant.

Jason was terrific, but my mother was the boss. He followed her rules. Sometimes I felt upset with him. I often thought he too had deserted me. Jason did whatever my mother told him to do. The years I spent living in their home were difficult for me. I never understood why I was there. I never felt loved by my mother.

My parents hired a live-in nanny, Yvonne, to take care of me. My mom and Jason would come home, shower, dress, and leave. There were times they wouldn't come back for days. Sometimes they would disappear for weeks. Yvonne became my family. She took better care of me than most of the people I stayed with in my life. I was very fond of her. She lived with us for several years. Like everyone else before her, one day she left. I cried like I did all the other times when people disappeared from my life. Sadly, I never saw her again.

Not long after she left, my mother came home one day and told me we were moving to Canada. It was my junior year of high school. I was sixteen and wanted to stay in school with my friends. I refused to go.

My parents owned our home, but we all agreed I couldn't live there by myself. It would be too costly for me to keep up on my own. My parents weren't happy about me staying behind. I was headstrong and I wasn't going anywhere. They could have fought me, but it wouldn't have done much good. In a year and a half, I would turn eighteen. I would be old enough to make my own decisions. I believe they expected I would fail if I stayed behind. I felt certain they thought that I would eventually move to Canada to live with them. I have no doubt that is why they refused to help me financially.

I think it was a turning point in my life. I moved into a one-bedroom apartment with five girls, a guy, a dog, and a cat. We didn't have much space, but we rarely noticed. The bond we formed was powerful. We each had a story. We were always there for one another. No matter what, the others came to the rescue. Our male roommate, Kevin, was a big brother figure. He loved us all and treated us like we were his sisters. Everyone got along beautifully. There were never any harsh words between us. We were all fighting for survival. We were like a support group living together. We all wanted to make a better life for ourselves. We had grown up beyond our years. By the time most of us had reached grade school, we had spent much of our time fending for ourselves.

I worked seven hours a day after school, five days a week, twelve hours on Saturday, and six hours on Sunday. All of us had busy schedules, but somehow we always found time to spend together.

My roommates and I had two wonderful years together. It was one of the greatest experiences of my life. They were the family I had picked for myself. After we graduated high school, everyone began going their separate ways. Three went on to college and one got a job out of state. Kevin married and I stayed behind, trying to figure out what I wanted to do. I think the time we spent together taught us the meaning of true friendship. We stayed close for many years. They became my telephone support group.

Fortunately, it didn't take long to find a new roommate. We rented a beautiful three-bedroom apartment on the south side. We had everything. I bought a car. Life was good for about a year. Then the company I worked for closed their doors and I lost my job. I didn't have money set aside for emergencies. Back then, I thought I would still be working for the same company today. That was the way I had grown up. We got a job and worked there for twenty years. Someday we retired with them. I didn't expect retirement to come so soon.

I began living off credit cards and started getting deeper and deeper into debt. Then I got meningitis and almost died. I couldn't work for a few months. The medical bills compounded my critical financial situation. I never wanted to call my parents to let them know I was in trouble. I could no longer afford to pay the rent, so I had to move out. I never thought being on my own would be so difficult.

I started bouncing around from friend to friend, staying for brief periods with each one. I was getting nervous about my future. I became very depressed. I was thousands of dollars in debt, homeless, and hungry. I was running out of friends who had enough room for me to stay with them. That's when I made the worst decision of my life. I decided I wanted to find my biological father.

My mother rarely spoke of him. She told me a few of the things that had happened. She asked me to stay away from him and to leave it alone. I blamed my mother that I didn't have a relationship with him. I was confident he had been looking for me his entire life. I always thought he must love me. I wanted to find him and get to know him. I was sure he must have been a nice person and knew he would be happy to see me. I had his family's last known address. I managed to find his sister, so I called and told her I wanted to see him. She called him and within a few hours, he called me.

"Hello, is this Daniella?" he said cautiously.

"Yes, it is."

My heart was pounding.

"This is your father."

I could hear the uneasiness in his voice. I tried to speak slowly and calmly.

"Thank you for calling me."

I was extremely nervous. I tried my best not to sound like a complete idiot.

"It's good to hear your voice. I have thought about you a lot through the years. I wondered if I would ever meet you," I confessed.

"Would you want to come up here for a visit? We could talk then," he said.

"Sure! Are you certain that would be all right

with you?"

I admit, it was embarrassing. I didn't have money for the trip. It was especially difficult since I was the one who wanted to see him.

"When would be good for you? I will make the arrangements."

I was deliriously happy. We spoke briefly a couple of times over the next few days. We firmed up my travel arrangements, and off I went. I was flying in on a Friday night and planned to stay until Sunday.

I had seen a photo of Nickie from when he was around twenty years old. I was sure he had changed a bit through the years. I wondered if I would recognize him. When I got off the plane, there were a lot of men waiting to meet people. I knew the moment I saw him that he was my father. He was older, but he still resembled his younger self. We walked toward each other, said hello, and shared an insignificant hug. We spent the rest of the time at the airport trying to get my luggage.

Nickie and I went downstairs to find his car, an older model Lincoln Town Car. We got in, and he started the car. He told me I would be staying at his home with his family. He spoke briefly about his wife, Nancy. Then Nickie went on to share a little about his three children. He glowed as he mentioned each one. I could tell Nickie loved them. For a moment, I tried to imagine what it would be like to have him in my life. My emotions were all over the place. Nickie was warm and friendly, but distant. I was patient and optimistic.

When we arrived at his home, I helped unpack the car. His wife, Nancy, was waiting when we got inside. She gave him a gentle kiss on the cheek. Their three kids came running down the stairs to meet me. I could tell they were very excited. They gave me a warm welcome. On that day, I met both of my half-brothers for the first time. I also met my half-sister, Nicole. She seemed happy to meet me. Later, she told me she had always wanted to meet her big sister. She bragged to her friends I was coming for a visit.

I had dinner with Nickie and his family that night. Then I went upstairs to Nicole's room, and we spent time getting to know each other. We were both boiling over with enthusiasm. We talked about school, boys, and sports. She shared her room with me that night. It was the nicest thing that had happened to me in a long time.

Early the next morning, we all went downstairs for breakfast. I sat in a chair close to where Nancy was cooking and spoke with her for a while. I enjoyed talking with her. I especially liked watching her cook. Everything came naturally to her. I always admired people who could make food taste fantastic, and they never used a measuring spoon, cup, or a cookbook. It was easy to understand why they preferred to eat at home.

Nickie told me at breakfast that the family had other things planned for the day. He thought if we spent the day alone together, it would give us a little time to get to know each other. It seemed like a good idea and I was looking forward to it.

"Daniella, dress warmly. I am going to take you to the racetrack today. Have you ever been to a racetrack?"

"No, it sounds like fun."

Within the hour, Nickie and I headed out. We tried to talk in the car on the way, but we couldn't seem to keep the conversation going. It was awkward. When we arrived at the track, Nickie parked the car. We got out and walked inside. Without saying a word, he went straight to the betting window to place his bet. I could tell when the race was over that he had lost money I didn't know how much, but he was not happy about it. Shortly after, we left. We hardly spoke a word during the ride back to his house.

Dinner was ready when we got to his home. We all sat around and talked about our day. I told everyone about my first time at a racetrack. I mostly spoke about the beautiful horses. I never mentioned Nickie's betting. After dinner, we all met downstairs in the family room, and we watched television for hours. I enjoyed hanging out with them that night.

We got up Sunday and went downstairs for breakfast. Nickie told us we would be staying in since the weather was dreary. All day, I kept thinking something was off. I wasn't sure what, but I had a bad feeling. We spent the day hanging out and watching television.

When it was time to take me to the airport, the kids wanted to go with us. Nickie insisted they stay behind. We said our tearful goodbyes, and off we went.

# Chapter Twenty

When we first got into the car, Nickie was quiet. Within a few minutes and without warning, the conversation took an ugly turn.

"So, did you have a nice time?" he asked.

"Yes, I did. Everyone was nice to me." I allowed my enthusiasm to show through.

"They are good kids," he said proudly.

"I liked them a lot," I said.

"I have been thinking about the possibilities since you got here. I asked myself about the future. I wondered if we should stay in touch. I have decided that wouldn't be a good idea."

I thought, *Could I have misunderstood what he said?* I know he saw the confusion on my face.

"I have to be honest. I was always curious about whether you were my kid. It was the only reason I invited you here. Your mother insisted she knew for a fact you were mine. I never believed her. In her line of work, how could she be certain?"

Within sixty seconds, he went from kind to cruel. I noticed a frightening difference in his demeanor. It took me a few minutes to understand what he was saying to me. I wondered if I had said something to upset him. Going back over our conversation in my mind, I couldn't come up with anything that would have caused such a drastic change in his behavior toward me.

"Her line of work? What do you mean, 'her line of work'?"

"Oh, come on, Daniella. Don't tell me you didn't know your mother was a whore," he chuckled.

"What are you saying?"

I was shocked. I could feel tears rolling down my face.

"My mother isn't a whore! She is married to my stepfather, Jason!"

"You can't be that stupid, little girl. I would have thought she would have had you turning tricks by now."

At that moment, I realized he was mentally twisted. He turned to me.

"The minute I saw you, I knew you were mine. You look just like my sister, Selena," he said with conviction.

At that point, I started to get angry.

"Stop! Let me out of this car."

I didn't care that it was freezing, snowing, or that I had no idea where we were. I just wanted to get away from Nickie. He didn't slow the car. He looked over and sneered at me with a wicked laugh.

"I am not stopping. I am taking you back to the airport. I want to make sure you get on the plane. I don't know why you came here, but you should have no reason to return. You said you were curious. Didn't your mother ever tell you curiosity killed the cat? I have a family. I don't need another one. You are nothing to me. I fucked your mother one night, and the next thing I knew the bitch was telling me she was pregnant. She fucked a lot of guys. What was I to think?"

At that point, I was crying uncontrollably. I

kept trying to pull myself together, but I couldn't. When we arrived at the airport, I jumped out of the car. A valet took my bags. Nickie walked around to my side and grabbed my arm. He leaned over and whispered in my ear.

"I bet you're a good fuck, just like your mother."

He grabbed my arm with a firm grip, then he yanked on it. He pushed me forward through the crowd at the airport. I wanted to scream, but I couldn't.

"I want to make sure you get on the plane. You better never show your face here again. Don't call. Don't write. Go home! Worst case, you'll turn out like your mother. She made a decent living. Look at all of the nice things she bought you when you were growing up."

I turned and looked at him, and all I saw was pure evil.

We arrived at the gate. Nickie got in my face and glared into my eyes. He shoved an envelope in my shirt pocket.

"Do not open it until the plane is off the ground."

He expressed himself in a way that made me

fearful of his every move. I wasn't about to do anything other than what he told me to do. I handed over my boarding pass and practically ran up the walkway to the plane. I moved quickly to get on and didn't look back. I was happy to be away from him. I found my seat, sat, and fastened my seatbelt. I continued to cry out loud. A female flight attendant walked over and wanted to know if I was okay. I asked for a glass of water and some tissues.

I wiped my tears and tried to regain control of my emotions. I was curious and anxious. What was in the envelope? As our plane began to taxi off to the runway, I pulled it from my pocket and opened it. There was a check inside for $4,000, made out to me. In those days, that was a lot of money. There was a note inside. He had written it in all capital letters: *TAKE THE MONEY. I OWE YOU THAT MUCH. DON'T EVER COME BACK. YOU ARE NOT WELCOME HERE.* He signed it, *Nickie*.

I stared at the words on the page in disbelief. I wanted to tear up the check and the note. I know I should have, but I didn't. I placed them back in the envelope and put it back in my shirt pocket. I felt certain I had just had an encounter with the devil himself. I wondered what I had been thinking. Why did I feel the need to meet this horrible creature? The floodgates opened and I cried incessantly. I finally fell asleep.

Eventually, the plane landed, and I got my luggage. I walked briskly to my car and tossed my luggage inside. I raced back to my friend's house. It felt like I drove forever. When I arrived, I ran inside, dropped my luggage on the floor, and immediately poured myself a glass of wine.

I tried to process everything Nickie said to me. I searched deep inside my soul for the truth. Could I have missed any signs through the years? I couldn't imagine. My mother and Jason seemed happy together. I could only recall one suspicious event. I never found out why my mom and Jason got into a fight, and my mother ended up with a bandage on her nose. I never understood why there was a For Sale sign in our yard the next morning. There had been nothing else that would have made me wonder whether there was any truth in anything Nickie said.

I couldn't imagine why Nickie would have said such things. I concluded the only reason was that he didn't want anything to do with me. Nickie wanted to guarantee I would never go back. I believed that he thought if he was mean enough to me, he could be sure I wouldn't contact him again. Nickie should have told me that when I called him. Instead, he waited until I got there. He let me meet and spend two days with my stepsister and stepbrothers. Then he told me on the way to the airport that he didn't want anything to do with me. The horrific things he said to me were unforgivable. I was emotionally exhausted. I eventually crawled into bed and cried myself to sleep.

I woke up the next day every bit as drained as I was the night before. Nothing made sense to me. I got up and showered and tried to plan my day. I couldn't stop thinking about what happened. I sat and drank my coffee while I continued to try to rationalize the events of the past few days.

I thought about the check Nickie gave me. I wanted to throw it away, but I was broke. After careful consideration, I decided to keep it. I justified it by telling myself Nickie was right. He owed me that much. I collected the bills I hadn't paid, pulled out my checkbook, and started writing checks to make the payments. I figured I would deposit the check, and it would clear by the time the merchants received their payment. I drove to the bank that morning. I deposited it into my checking account and dropped my payments at the post office.

By then, I was in a much better mood. I was whole again. I still had money to get an apartment and hold me over for a few weeks. I knew I needed to continue feverishly looking for a job. At that moment, I was feeling good about the trip I had taken. I was financially sound. I was glad he had given me the check. I didn't know what I would have done without it. The fact that I could use it to regain my financial stability made it easier to forget some of the horrible things that had happened.

Although the meeting ended painfully, I finally had closure. I knew why my mother had told me to leave it alone. He was a disgusting human being. I couldn't imagine what she ever saw in him. I was glad she had divorced him. I dreaded the thought of having this horrible person as a father.

I spent every day looking for work. Sadly, once again, I had to move. My friend's sister was coming home from college and they needed her room. I continued to go from one friend to another. I kept looking for work. I was spending the money faster than I expected, and I was fearful of running out before I could find a roommate and a job. I moved several times. This time, I was staying with one of my old roommates. Vickie said I could stay with her for a while. She was at work one day when there was a knock on the door, and I opened it. There stood one of the friends I had stayed with weeks before. I was shocked. I invited her inside.

"Hello, Susan! What are you doing here?" She looked upset.

"How did you find me? What's wrong?"

I hadn't told her where I was staying. I couldn't believe she found me.

"Daniella, I thought I had better let you know, a couple of police officers stopped by my apartment. They were looking for you."

Susan appeared perplexed, and so was I. I wondered why on earth police officers would be looking for me. I had never even gotten a parking or speeding ticket. I couldn't imagine what I could have done wrong.

"Daniella, I asked them why they needed to see you, but they wouldn't tell me. They just said they needed to speak with you on a private matter."

She was noticeably worried.

"I won't tell them where you are staying. I promise. Just be careful, because you weren't that hard to find."

I am sure she could tell I was both concerned and anxious to find out what was happening.

"I didn't get a good feeling about it," said Susan.

She paused, and then she looked at me with concern. "I need to go. Let me know if you find out anything."

I opened the door and Susan leaned in and kissed me on the cheek. I watched her walk to her car and drive away.

The entire day, I pondered over what to do. Then that evening, I started receiving calls from other friends. They were the ones that I had previous stayed with, and each one of them shared a similar story. A couple of police officers visited them, and they were looking for me. My concern was quickly turning to panic. I considered what I thought was one strong possibility. Could they want to ask me about Nickie? He was such an awful person. My mother had rarely spoken of him, but she would make an occasional comment. I recall her saying he was a big gambler. I thought it might have been possible someone found out that I had visited him. Could they believe that I had seen or heard something?

My mind continued to race. I went to bed later than usual but hardly slept. In the morning, I could think of nothing else. I considered many things I might do to find out what was going on. I was quickly becoming afraid to deal with the issue on my own. I thought long and hard about who I could call to help me. I knew there was only one person I could depend on who lived nearby. His name was Rick. We had been friends since I was twelve. I didn't want to bother him, so I hesitated to call. I decided to rest and see how I felt the next day.

# Chapter Twenty-one

*I* was becoming more concerned each day. I finally broke down and called my friend Rick. He was someone I trusted completely. No matter what the issue, he always helped me. I told him about the calls I had received from my friends and about the one who came looking for me. They each had similar stories about the police wanting to speak to me. For a moment Rick got quiet. I could tell he was concerned. He assured me I shouldn't worry, but the tone of his voice was saying something else.

"We're going to the police station. I will be

there to pick you up in thirty minutes. We need to find out why they are interested in you. I am only guessing that they may want to ask if you have information about someone else. You can't continue to be afraid, so we need to find out what is going on."

Rick was convincing.

I dressed and waited for Rick. When I heard a knock on the door, I was certain it was him. He was always on time, and this time was no different. I opened the door, saw him, and burst into tears. He put his arms around me and tried to comfort me.

"Don't worry. I won't let you go through this by yourself. I will be there for you."

He gave me a giant hug. I wiped my tears, and off we went. It took about thirty minutes to get to the police station. When we arrived and got out of the car, Rick put his arms around me and gave me another hug.

"Please, don't be afraid. I am sure it is nothing."

The idea of walking into a police station to ask why they were looking for me terrified me.

We walked inside and went up to the front desk. A female police officer in uniform sat there. The nameplate on her shirt read, Jazmine Riley.

She had cropped black hair. When she stood up, you could tell she was very muscular. The uniform made her appear masculine. She was intimidating.

"Good afternoon, Officer Riley. My name is Rick Summers. I am here with my friend Daniella DeChristopher. Several of Daniella's friends told her the police have been asking around about her. We thought we had better come down here and find out why."

Rick always had a kind way of speaking to people.

"Have a seat in the lobby. I will check into it. Give me a moment, please."

She had no expression whatsoever. She scanned me with her eyes from top to bottom. It seemed invasive, but I was in no position to ask her if there was an issue. She stepped away from the front desk. With a bit of an attitude, she walked through a door in the back of the room.

Within minutes, she returned. Another police officer was with her. He had on a police uniform, but he was very rugged looking. The male officer looked in my direction, and I could see he had a very serious look on his face. Rick and I stood. Both police officers walked toward me as if they were trying to block me. I began to feel threatened. Within seconds, I realized something was wrong. The male police officer got within a couple of feet of me and entered my space. It was uncomfortable and scary. I started to panic and cry.

"What's wrong? Rick, what's going on?"

Rick tried to get between the male police officer and me.

"Step back! You cannot interfere with police business. Sit down unless you want to go to jail with her!"

Rick stepped back and I could see fear on his face.

"Don't worry, Daniella. We will get to the bottom of this. Please remain calm."

The female police officer looked directly into my eyes.

"Turn around and place your hands behind your back."

I was shocked and dazed. I didn't understand what was happening to me.

"Now!" she shouted.

I felt the blood rush to my head. I felt weak at the knees. By this time, I was crying profusely.

"Rick, what is going on? Help me! Do something!"

Rick started getting angry.

"Why are you treating her this way? We came here to find out why you were looking for her. Don't do this! What is the issue? Please!"

The female police officer placed handcuffs on me.

"Turn back around," she commanded.

"Why are you doing this to me?" I cried.

The female police officer spoke in a firm voice.

"There are eighteen outstanding warrants for your arrest for writing worthless checks. Under Florida Statute 832.05, writing worthless checks for more than fifty dollars is a felony in the state of Florida. Therefore, you are under arrest."

She lacked any emotion or compassion.

"What are you talking about?"

I was shocked. I was certain the police had me confused with someone else.

"You have the wrong person. I didn't write any bad checks. There must be some mistake. Call my bank. I will prove it. I have money in my account. I didn't write any bad checks!"

At that moment, I believed in my innocence.

"Daniella, you need to call your bank. They are one of the ones who pressed charges against you," she replied.

"That's crazy!"

Rick kept telling me to calm down.

"You're not going anywhere. You are under arrest. You will be here until we complete the booking process. Eventually, your friend can post your bond. If no one bonds you out, you will have to appear before a magistrate judge."

The male police officer turned to me and began to read me my Miranda rights. I felt like my mind separated from my body.

"You have the right to remain silent. Anything you say can and will be used against you in a court of law. You have the right to an attorney."

There was more, but my mind went blank. I didn't hear another word.

"Daniella, I have never let you down. I won't now," Rick said with conviction. "You need to calm down. We will figure this out. I will get you out of here. I promise!"

By this time, I could see the concern on Rick's face.

"Be nice to her! She is a good girl. Something

io wrong here. She is not a criminal. Could you show her a little compassion?" he begged.

At that point, I was crying so hard I couldn't hear anything anyone was saying to me. The female police officer started guiding me toward a door in the back of the room.

"Daniella, we need some help. Don't worry. I will be back as soon as possible. Quiet, calm down."

Rick's hands were moving in a way to get me to regain control of my emotions and stop crying.

"She will be here. There is a bail bondsman across the street. You can bail her out once we complete the booking process. We should be done here in a couple of hours," said the male police officer.

"Please calm down, Daniella. I need for you to be strong."

I watched Rick walk toward the front door and out of the building. I had never felt so afraid and helpless in my life. It was the most horrible thing I had ever experienced.

The female police officer directed me through several doors. We finally arrived at the booking area, where they took photos and fingerprinted me. I could feel my body trembling. We walked down a hallway with wall-to-wall cells. The police officer paused, and then she stopped and pushed a button. A barred gate opened. She took the handcuffs off me, escorted me inside, and exited the cell. The sound of the door slamming sealed my fears. I felt numb and confused. She locked the door behind her. I walked over to a bed and collapsed and cried. Within a few minutes, I passed out from exhaustion.

A guard woke me up later that day. She walked up to my cell door and unlocked it.

"DeChristopher, you are free to go. Your friend Rick bailed you out."

She walked me to the front. The minute I saw Rick, I rushed toward him.

"Let's get out of here," he said.

We hurried toward the car.

"Get in."

He was barely in the car when he started rambling.

"I went to the bail bondsman. I didn't have enough money to get you out. I had to run around and collect money from friends. Then I had to go to the bank and cash the checks," he said.

"How much was it?" I asked.

"Don't worry about that now. We will get most

of it back when this is over. We are going to stop by my house and call your bank. I want to let them know you are coming in. We don't need any more drama today. We can head straight there after we alert them we are coming. We are going to find out what is going on."

It seemed like a good plan to me. We stopped by Rick's and I stayed in the car. Then we headed to the bank, a fifteen-minute drive away. We walked inside and up to the receptionist, Denise.

"Good morning, my name is Rick Summers. I am here with Daniella DeChristopher. We have a four o'clock appointment with the branch manager, Mr. Simmons," said Rick.

"Yes, he is expecting you. Please have a seat. I will let him know you are here," said Denise.

A man entered the room. He looked very distinguished. He was wearing a classic dark blue suit and wasn't much taller than me. I guessed he was around fifty years old. He had thin salt and pepper hair. We introduced ourselves.

"Please be seated. Thank you for calling. I printed Daniella's bank statement. I wanted to see if I could figure out what happened. On May twenty-fifth, there was a deposit made of four thousand dollars. We received eighteen checks after the deposit. Unfortunately, the four-thousand-dollar check did not clear."

I began trying to process what he was saying.

"What do you mean, the check did not clear?" I asked.

I know he must have noticed the puzzled look on my face.

"Just what I said, Daniella. It didn't clear."

He seemed confused by my response.

"That's impossible. The check was given to me by my father," I exclaimed.

He looked at me with curiosity.

"Your father?"

"Yes, he gave me the check. Look at the name on the check. That's my father's name and signature."

He looked puzzled.

"I am sorry to hear that Daniella. The check was worthless."

I sat there and thought about what he was saying to me. I tried to sort it out in my mind. Then suddenly it became crystal clear. I looked at Rick and burst into tears. Rick leaned over to comfort me. He thanked the manager for his time and assured him we would take care of it.

"As you can see, Daniella had no idea. It was not intentional. We will figure this out, and she will pay back everything everyone is owed "

I was sure the manager could see we were sincere.

"It has been a very long and painful day for Daniella. I need to get her home. We will be in touch."

We got up and walked out. Rick held me as we walked out the door, and I cried all the way to the car.

"I am sorry this happened to you, Daniella."

Rick tried to comfort me. He held me until I finally stopped crying.

# Chapter
## Twenty-two

inally, my attorney notified me a hearing date had been scheduled. Everyone met in the judge's chambers. Rick went with me. We sat quietly when the judge spoke. Then he gave me an opportunity to tell my side of the story.

"Daniella DeChristopher?"

"Yes, Your Honor."

"You are facing five years in jail and full restitution. You will need to cover the four thousand dollars in merchant checks, pay court costs, bank fees, and merchant fees."

"Your Honor, my father gave me the check."

"Your father?"

He looked at me with confusion.

"Yes, Your Honor. I went to see him for the first time. He told me he didn't want anything to do with me. He gave me the check and told me to go away. I was broke, homeless, and hungry. I was running out of places to stay. I deposited the check into my bank account, paid my bills, and bought groceries. I didn't know the check wasn't any good."

I spoke with sincerity.

"If what you are saying is true, that concerns me. I will be ordering a PSI. I will decide your fate after I have received the report."

"What is a PSI?" I asked.

"Presentence investigation. We will be checking your school records, employment records, and speaking to various friends and family members. The information we receive will help us to make a final decision about what to do with you."

The judge slammed his gavel on his desk, and that was it. We exited the building and headed home.

About a month later, the attorney called me to say that they had completed the PSI. He told me I would need to reappear before the judge in his chambers. The judge seemed friendly when we arrived, so I felt more comfortable than I had previously.

"Daniella, we investigated the events you presented to us. We did a PSI, as I told you we would. We were successful in verifying the information you gave us. We asked various individuals about you. Everyone we interviewed said you are a lovely young woman. Your school records show you were an A/B student. Your English teacher reported he had spent time with you to help you polish your writing skills. I understand he thinks you have potential as a writer. You have excelled in sports. Your employers said you were an excellent worker. How did you find the time to do so many things and do them all so well?"

The judge shook his head and chuckled.

I sat patiently and listened.

"The results of these discoveries are why I am having such a hard time with this. Did you know your father was on probation?"

"No, Your Honor. I don't know anything about him except he wrote me a bad check," I explained.

The judge looked at me with grave concern.

"He keeps company with some very bad people. He has been in and out of prison his entire life for various crimes. He also has a gambling problem."

I recalled the day Nickie took me to the racetrack. The judge had confirmed my suspicions. He lost money that day that he couldn't afford to lose.

The judge looked straight into my eyes. He spoke with compassion.

"Daniella. It saddens me to tell you this, but I think you should know. Not only was the check he gave you worthless, but the bank had closed the account two years prior. Your biological father knowingly gave you a fraudulent check. For me, that is especially disturbing," he said.

At that moment, I felt the blood rush to my head. I was angry beyond words but tried not to show it.

"I cannot understand what kind of man would do this to his daughter. I believe this is one of the most difficult cases with which I have had to render a decision," he said.

I could see the concern on his face. It was genuine. He shook his head in disbelief.

"I have thought long and hard about what to do with you, and there doesn't seem to be a simple answer. Based on the information we discovered, I cannot in good conscience put you in jail. Your only crime was not letting the check clear. However, I cannot ignore your failure to do so."

"Your Honor, it never crossed my mind he would give me a bad check."

"I understand," he said sympathetically. "Many people were hurt by these actions. Unfortunately, you must make restitution."

The rest was hard for me to hear.

"That is why I hereby sentence you to probation for two years or whatever time it takes for you to pay full restitution. The terms of your probation are as follows. You must pay back all the money through gainful employment. You will have a probation officer assigned to you, and you will give your weekly employment checks to your probation officer. The probation officer will make the necessary payments for you. The probation officer will notify the court when you have paid your debt in full. We will schedule a court date. Upon completion of the requirements, this court will expunge all charges against you associated with this case. Do you understand the seriousness of the charges against you? Do you have any questions about any of the terms as I have stated them to you?"

"No, Your Honor. I understand them," I said humbly.

He delivered his final statement with conviction: "Then I trust you will conduct yourself accordingly."

"Yes, Your Honor, I will."

I made every effort to stay calm, but I could feel the blood rush to my head again. I wanted to get a gun, drive north, knock on Nickie's door, and shoot him dead. I was having trouble concentrating.

"May I go home now, Your Honor?"

I wanted to get out of there as fast as I could. The judge looked at me and responded.

"That is not going to happen, Daniella. I believe you need to stay here tonight," he commanded.

I was shocked.

"I don't understand. What are you saying?"

"I think it would be best for everyone if you spend the night in county jail."

"Why?" I pleaded.

I was terrified.

The judge looked at a police officer standing by the back door.

"Take her to the jail. She will stay there tonight. I will consider letting her go home tomorrow," the judge commanded.

"Your Honor, why? Please let me go home. I am fine," I begged.

"Not tonight, dear. Tonight, you will be in custody. I will let you know in the morning whether or not you can go home tomorrow."

I cried as they escorted me out of the judge's chambers. The police officer stopped for a moment. He told me to turn around and put my hands behind my back; then he handcuffed me. Rick stood and watched them take me out of the room. At that moment, I hated everyone, including Rick.

# Chapter Twenty-three

*I* was released the next day. My emotions were all over the place, but I pulled myself together and began looking for a job. I found two. I started both jobs the following week. I worked during the day at an automobile dealership, and I waitressed at an Italian restaurant at night and on weekends. I wanted to pay back the money I owed as quickly as I could. I desperately wanted to get out of trouble.

My probation officer's name was Jessie. She had no personality, or if she did, I never saw it. I don't recall ever seeing her smile. Jessie was not feminine. She had short dark brown hair and an ordinary face. She was average height and weight, but she had a commanding presence when she entered the room. She had previously worked as a high school security guard and a truancy officer. Reining in young adults seemed to be her specialty.

Both of my employers knew I was on probation. Jessie met with each of them. She stopped by the automobile dealership every Friday afternoon to see me. She was a rigid female officer and it was clear her intention was to intimidate me. She was doing an excellent job. She often made unannounced visits. If I stayed in the restroom too long, my employer would call her. Jessie wanted to know every move I made. She made living a normal life difficult.

About eighteen months later, I was beginning to struggle to keep up the pace. An acquaintance told me he had something that could help me. It turned out to be a little black pill. I needed the energy to keep me going and was willing to take anything if it would help me. I started taking them. In the beginning, I took them when I needed energy. Then I started taking one with my morning coffee. Within a short period, I was relying on the pills to get me through each day. Since I was racing on black beauties during the day, I needed something to help me sleep at night, so I started using over-the-counter sleep aids.

Judge Sanderson and his wife came into the restaurant where I worked at least once a week, and I would wait on them. They often invited me to sit with them for a short time. Even when they ordered only coffee, the judge would always leave me a twenty-dollar tip. He became a wonderful mentor to me, and I grew fond of him. His wife was a beautiful person, and her kindness showed through. The judge often shared interesting stories. Most of them were inspirational. I was always happy to see him and his lovely wife.

My probation officer came to the restaurant one day and told me I had paid everything I owed. I was ecstatic. A few weeks later, I received a notice of hearing in the judge's chambers. I was anxious and nervous. Rick went with me, as he always had before. When we walked into the courthouse, we were escorted to Judge Sanderson's chambers.

"Hello, Daniella! Please, you and Rick have a seat. I understand you have paid full restitution. That is excellent news!"

He called his secretary, Janie, over.

"Janie, I want you to send a certified letter to Nickie Demetrios."

He had my attention.

"I think it would be a good day to add a significant amount of stress to his life."

"What would you like for the letter to say?" Janie asked.

"*See you in court.* Give it to me. I will sign it," the judge said.

"Daniella, you don't have the time or resources to travel out of state to pursue the fraudulent check, nor would I allow it. However, I think a notice from a judge telling Nickie Demetrios we will see him in court should scare the daylights out him," he chuckled.

"Your biological father is on probation. Let him think we are going to pursue the worthless check issue. I am hoping it will cause him many sleepless nights."

We all saw the humor in the judge's plan.

"Daniella, I need for you to know this was a difficult case for me. The more I got to know you, the harder it got. I see many nice people with bad breaks come through this door. They often walk out of here mad at the world. The odds are favorable they will be back. I could see the pain on your face. I didn't want that to happen to you. A night in jail, probation, and restitution must have seemed harsh to you. It was the only way I could keep an eye on you. I needed to be in control of where you went and what you did. I felt it was necessary. I saw the anger in your eyes and the hatred on your face. I bet you wanted to drive to Nickie's house and shoot him dead."

We all chuckled. Judge Sanderson knew exactly what I was thinking.

"I promised you I would expunge your record if you fulfilled the terms of your probation. Janie, please bring me the largest metal trash container you can find."

She brought one over and placed it next to the judge's desk.

"Daniella, this is your file." He raised it from his desk.

"These are the only records that exist of the past two years of your life. Would you like to do the honors?"

I got up, smiled, and walked over. Judge Sanderson handed me a cigarette lighter and the file. I placed the file over the trash can and set the edge of the folder on fire. I placed it inside. We all watched it burn. There wasn't a dry eye in the room.

"Daniella don't let the events of the past two years ruin your life. You have too much going for you. Dust yourself off and continue forward. I know you have the strength and courage to make things happen. You don't need anyone to do things for you. I have no doubt you can do them for yourself," he said with passion.

"I want to hear good reports. I will be keeping an eye on you. I intend to stop over and have my nice Italian dinners from time to time. I want to see your smiling face there."

I blushed.

"If you ever need someone to talk to, I am here for you. I don't want to see you in my chambers ever again. I have faith in you. Don't disappoint me. Be well!"

We all stood up and said our goodbyes. It was a joyous day! I was free again. My date with hell had ended. It had been one of the worst experiences of my life, but I learned many things. I had met a judge with a beautiful heart. I found out Rick was truly the friend I thought he was. I learned I should have listened to my mother. Too bad for me I learned it the hard way.

I no longer needed or wanted to take the black beauties. Unfortunately, I figured out in a short time it was out of my control. I couldn't stop taking them. I couldn't get out of bed unless I did. I stayed with Rick for the next few months, and he helped me go through withdrawal. The withdrawal was much harder than I ever imagined, but I finally got through it.

I promised myself I would never take another pill that wasn't prescribed by a doctor. It was one of the most distressing phases of my entire life. I never wanted to go through anything like it again. I was slowly beginning to feel like my old self. It was such an incredible feeling. I discovered youth often helps us to heal and move on.

I found a good job with a bank check company. I thought it was funny I would end up working for a company that printed checks. I got a new boyfriend and we moved in together. I thought we would live happily ever after. Unfortunately, as with a lot of stories in my life, it didn't end as well as I had planned. I spent my time working hard to create a decent life for us. He spent his time cheating on me every chance he got. I finally had enough and kicked him out of my apartment. I was glad he was gone, but I struggled with the thought of being alone again. I felt depressed and stayed in bed for days trying to sort out my life. I took long naps and spent endless hours dreaming and planning my future. I carefully examined my options.

We had been separated for only a few weeks when I received a knock on my door. I opened it and two police officers were standing in front of me.

"Daniella DeChristopher?"

"Yes," I responded.

"You need to come with us to the police station."

"For what?"

"You are wanted for questioning regarding an assault on Nickie Demetrios."

I am certain that I didn't look upset.

"Someone assaulted that SOB?" I chuckled. "I hope you don't think I had something to do with it. I guess he ticked off the wrong person this time. I wish I had known. I would have loved to have been there. Unfortunately, no one told me anything about it."

"You expect us to believe you don't know

anything about the crime?" she said.

"I just told you I don't know anything about it. I still speak to Nickie's sister from time to time. Nickie loves to gamble. I heard he had gambled away the inheritance he got from his father's department store. You should question some of his gambling buddies. Besides, I have no doubt he has a lot of enemies. He is that kind of guy."

They didn't seem impressed by my response or my reaction.

"We need for you to come with us. I think we should ask you these questions downtown."

"My pleasure. I don't have anything to hide."

I grabbed my purse and locked up. I walked alongside the police officers. One of them opened the back door of the patrol car and I slid into the backseat. We didn't speak a word on the way to the police station.

Not long after we got there, they placed me in a holding room. I told the officers I didn't think they could detain me unless they charged me with something. A female officer came into the room. She started asking me the same questions.

"Did you know about the crime against Nickie Demetrios?"

"No, I did not."

"Daniella, this is your chance to come clean. Did you hire someone to cause harm to Nickie Demetrios?"

"No, I did not."

The grilling went on for hours.

"I will not apologize for not being upset that someone hurt that SOB. I would have done it myself if I had the courage."

At this point, my anger and frustration were beginning to show through.

"Again, I have no knowledge of anything concerning Nickie Demetrios. I will not apologize for not caring if that horrible human being is dead or alive."

By this time, I was exhausted.

"Where were you on the night of May 15th?"

"May 15th? I have no clue. What day was May 15th?" I asked.

"It was a Tuesday," she said.

"Tuesday? I work on Tuesdays," I explained.

"Did you work that Tuesday?" she asked.

"I haven't had a day off this year. Yes, I worked on that Tuesday. Call my employer."

They kept asking me the same questions.

"Either let me out of here or let me call an attorney. I have had enough of these ridiculous questions."

I continued to try to make them understand.

"Am I being charged with a crime?"

There was complete silence.

"One phone call, that's it," said the male officer.

That's when I called Billy.

The female officer escorted me to a cell. There I sat anxiously awaiting Billy's arrival. I lay on the bed, where I continued to drift in and out of sleep. I was exhausted.

# Chapter
# Twenty-four

The tall, skinny female guard walked up to my cell door.

"Good afternoon, Daniella. Your attorney is here."

She opened the door. We walked down the hall to the front. There stood Billy. I had no doubt I was visibly nervous.

He was standing with his back toward me. He turned around when he heard the door open. He had grown into a handsome, sophisticated man. I knew he saw me. I waited to see his response. He opened his arms and I raced toward him. He put his arms around me. I tried hard to compose myself, but I was a wreck.

"Let's get out of here," he said.

We walked briskly out the door and down the steps. When I reached the sidewalk, I started laughing. Parked at the curb was a beautiful late-model red Mustang convertible. I knew it was Billy's.

"You still have this old Mustang? It is beautiful!"

He had kept it in mint condition. It brought back many good memories. He opened the door, I got in, and we drove away.

"Don't call her old. She is sensitive. Her name is Betsy. I stopped by the house to pick her up. I knew you would get a kick out of seeing her," he said, smiling

We looked at each other with genuine affection.

"We are going to get you cleaned up. Then we are going to have a nice lunch. You are going to tell me all about you and how you ended up here. Then I am going to work on getting this fixed," he said.

I knew he would. You can never break a real bond between two people.

Billy and I stopped by the apartment. No one

was home. I showered and dressed, and we headed for lunch. It was a joyous time. We reminisced, then spent hours talking about what had happened. Afterward, he dropped me back at the apartment, assuring me that he would be in touch.

A few days later, Billy stopped by. Rick was at my place, and I introduced them to each other. We sat at the breakfast table and I made us coffee. We made small talk for a while. Then Billy brought us up to date. He spoke with conviction.

"I did some research. I don't think the police had any evidence to connect you with the crime against your father."

"No disrespect, but don't call him my father. Please refer to him as Nickie," I said.

"Understood," said Billy. "I am trying to find out why they thought they could detain you. Daniella, I must ask you. I know he did terrible things to you and I know you despise him. I need to know if you had anything to do with someone inflicting bodily harm on Nickie. I need to know if you had any knowledge of someone committing the crime against him. You need to tell me. It is confidential. It is the only way I can provide you with proper counsel," he said, begging for honesty.

I looked straight into his beautiful blue eyes.

"Billy, I promise that man is of no interest to me. I don't care if he lives or dies. I wouldn't waste another minute of my life on that horrible excuse for a man. He means nothing to me."

I was passionate in my delivery.

"I am sorry, Daniella. I had to ask. The police know you have hard feelings against him. That is why they questioned you. I don't think they had enough evidence to press charges against you. I think they thought you would break down and confess. I checked and they haven't signed an arrest warrant. If they had, I believe you would have heard from them by now. I doubt you will hear from them again."

I knew I could count on Billy. Even as a young boy, his loyalty was uncompromising.

We sat around and talked for hours. Billy and Rick seemed to enjoy telling funny stories about me. I didn't always see the humor in them. We had a lovely time sharing our affection for one another. We stood, said our goodbyes, and hugged. Rick and I walked Billy to the door and watched him walk to his car. We waved as he pulled away.

I continued trying to rebuild my life. It had

been in shambles for several years. I tried not to think much about the past. Instead, I decided to move forward with my future. Things were gradually coming together for me. It had been a year since the police had questioned me. I decided it was time to call and follow up with Billy.

"Hello, Billy. It's Daniella. Thank you for taking my call. It's been a while since we spoke. I wanted to touch base with you about what happened. I was wondering if there is anything I should be doing at this point. It has been a year. I haven't heard anything from anyone."

"Daniella, if you haven't heard anything by now, they either solved the case, or they just couldn't find enough evidence to arrest you."

He assured me I shouldn't worry.

"Go on with your life. If they contact you again, let me know. I will always be here for you."

We talked about having lunch soon and promised we would stay in touch. I felt I had the closure I was looking for to move forward.

After my conversation with Billy, I made a few calls to share my news and excitement. When I was done, I walked briskly to my car. I was eager to drive into the sunset and away from all that had happened. I opened the car door, got in, and placed the key in the ignition. I put the top down, turned on my favorite music station, and began driving. I loved the feeling of the wind on my face and the breeze blowing through my hair. I took a scenic drive on winding roads.

I pondered my life. I thought about my biological father, Nickie, my mother, and my stepfather. I realized the complexity of the family I had inherited. I thought about all the people I knew with loving families, and I was a bit sad that my life had been so fragmented. I refused to feel sorry for myself. I knew I would survive one way or the other. I had gotten this far, and I had no choice but to continue forward.

There was a place where I often went to look out over the city. I was heading there. I saw the side road just after I made a curve. I could see the area where I usually parked. I pulled in and turned off the ignition. I felt more relaxed than I had in years. The temperature was comfortable outside, and there wasn't a cloud in the sky. I sat back and looked up at the moon and the stars. I loved the bright lights. It was the perfect night. I closed my eyes and prayed for a moment of peace. I dozed off.

I was awakened by bright headlights shining in my rearview mirror. A vehicle pulled in behind me. I heard the engine shut off, and I could see the car door open. A large man was walking toward me. He walked up to the passenger's side, opened the door, and got in. It was Big Al. I leaned over and kissed him on the cheek

"Hello, Daniella. It's been much too long since I have seen you. You have turned into a beautiful young woman. How are you doing?"

I wanted to freeze that moment in time. There I sat looking out at the city, and Big Al was sitting next to me.

"It's nice here. I like the view," said Big Al.

"Me, too. Whenever I feel a little lost, I park here. It's peaceful."

Big Al reached over and placed his hand over mine.

"I want you to know. It was excruciating, but there won't be any permanent damage," said Big Al.

"It's okay, Al. I would rather not know the details."

I sat back and closed my eyes and took a deep breath. I felt a calm come over my body. Then I reached into the backseat and pulled out a large black bag.

"Here's the money I owe you. I had it packaged in hundred-dollar bills."

"No way, Daniella. This one is a gift from me and the boys. You mean the world to us. What Nickie did to you was reprehensible. Don't ever feel bad about any of this. Go on with your life."

I could feel his love, and I knew he was speaking from his heart.

"That SOB deserved what he got. He is lucky to be alive. There are a few of the boys who would have liked for it to have ended differently."

We shared a devious chuckle.

"We will always love you and your mother. I know she is a tough lady. Don't be too hard on her. She did the best she could under the circumstances. You have no idea the heartbreak she has endured in her life. Your mother was a broken woman by the time she was twenty. She was so proud of you when you left home. She told us you got an apartment. She bragged about you every time one of the guys spoke to her. I believe she loves you in her own way. I know she doesn't always show it. I don't think your mother is willing to open herself up for more disappointment. Love has never ended well for her.

Your mother did what she had to do. She didn't have any other choice. Please trust me when I tell you, she did it for you. She tried hard to limit your exposure to her life."

I could see he was trying to be diplomatic and make me understand.

"No matter what you might think, she helped to make you the beautiful person you are today. She sheltered you a lot more than you know. I hope you will someday find a place in your heart to forgive her. Your mother isn't a bad person. Life has not been kind to her. Heartbreak and disappointment consumed her life."

Big Al was always sincere.

"Keep doing what you are doing. Build a life for yourself and don't ever look back. Don't let these events destroy the life your mother worked so hard to save. Be happy."

I sat quietly, carefully considering every word he said to me.

"I need for you to know that anytime you need us, we will always be here for you. We love you like a daughter. If anyone ever messes with you, just let us know."

There had always been a strong bond

between Big Al, the boys, and me. I would never forget the wonderful time we had spent in Miami when I was just a little girl. I was confident Big Al meant every word he was saying.

"I have to go. I need to take care of some business. Be well and be happy! The guys asked me to give you a little present from us."

It was a surprise, and I was humbled. Big Al handed me a small box. I removed the wrapping paper and opened it. It was a diamond heart necklace. It was magnificent. I couldn't conceal my emotions. As tears rolled down my face, I thanked him and asked him to thank the boys for me.

"It's symbolic. The boys want you to know you will always be in their hearts."

We were both choked up. I gave Big Al a long loving hug, then we said our goodbyes. He got out of the car and stood at my window for a moment. We looked at each other. Big Al headed back to his car, and I watched him get in and drive away. He looked back and threw me a kiss, and I did the same.

It was time for me to go home. I rubbed my eyes. I got out of the car for a moment and stretched my legs. I got back in and put the top up. I started the car and drove away. It had been a long day, and

I was anxious to get home and go to bed. The next morning, I got up and showered, dressed, and planned my day. It was especially important, because this would be the first day of my new life.

While I was consumed with thoughts and dreams of harming Nickie for what he did to me, I knew in my heart I could never do it. I would lie in bed at night and try to think of something that would cause him great pain. On many occasions, I even considered hiring someone else to bring harm to him. As much as it was what I wanted, I knew I could never hurt someone or be responsible for hurting someone. That night, I decided that I was going to stop obsessing about hurting Nickie and start concentrating on rebuilding my life.

# Chapter
## Twenty-five

*I* had survived a life of deceit, pain, and suffering. I was twenty-six and ready for a fresh start. I wanted to put the events of my past behind me. I made the decision to accept a transfer to South Florida with my employer.

When someone asked about my childhood, I told them I had grown up in North Florida. My mother and stepfather raised me. I never shared any of the details of my past, worried that if people found out, they would think less of me. I had low self-esteem. My parents hadn't loved me, so why would anyone else? I didn't think I deserved someone nice.

Instead, I made bad choices. My insecurities drove me to spend time with people who were in no position to judge me. I ended up in destructive relationships. I allowed people to take advantage of my kindness.

Years later, I received a call from Nickie's sister, Selena. It was Thanksgiving morning. She told me Nickie was dying. She didn't expect him to make it through the day. Selena said Nickie had asked to speak with me. I told her I didn't have any reason to talk to him. I told her to tell him to take it up with the big guy upstairs. A few hours later, Selena called to let me know Nickie had died. I felt nothing.

My stepfather, Jason, died when I was thirty-five. I had always thought he was the glue that held my mother and me together. As time went by, she and I drifted further apart. We hadn't spoken for years. I often wondered if she ever moved back into our old house. I was forty-five when her boyfriend called me.

"Is this Daniella DeChristopher?" he asked.

"Who is this?"

"My name is Frank Mason. I am looking for Daniella DeChristopher. This telephone number is the last one I had for her. I am her mother's companion. I need to reach Daniella on an urgent matter."

"Frank, this is Daniella. What's wrong?"

I gasped for air.

"Your mother has been diagnosed with terminal lung cancer. You need to come home. She is asking for you."

I packed and went home that year to take care of her. The moment I saw her, we put our arms around each other. We held each other like we never had before. She looked frail and she was carrying a small oxygen tank with her. We spent hours sitting and talking about life and death. We both searched deep within to find good memories. We reminisced about the fun times we'd had together and didn't speak about the other stuff.

We never spoke a word about Nickie. He was a sensitive subject. My mother could never get over the fact that she had told me to leave it alone, and I didn't. She said she thought I deserved what I got for not listening to her. I desperately wanted to tell my mother about all the dreams I'd had through the years, about Big Al and the boys doing horrible things to Nickie, but I thought it would be best if I didn't mention his name.

We talked about Gina. My mother wished they had stayed in touch. One day we spent hours sifting through old records, trying to find telephone numbers connected to Gina. We wanted to call her. We both wanted to tell Gina how much we had missed her through the years. I believe my mother wanted to say goodbye and thank Gina for her friendship. We tried our best, but we couldn't find her. Hopefully, someday Gina will read this book and realize how much she meant to my mother and me.

One of the most heartbreaking experiences of my life was spending time with my mother while she was dying. I stayed with her for more than a year before she passed. I felt intense love and sadness for her during the months we were together. I regretted that there had been such a distance between us. In my mother's final days, she told me she wasn't afraid to die. She said she had many regrets in her life, but life hadn't given her choices. She did what she'd had to do to survive and raise a child on her own. I buried her the following July. Only a handful of people came to say goodbye.

I spent days packing up her home. I kept a

few special pieces and the rest I sold or gave away. I found a box of old tax records. I opened it, and there were at least ten years of tax records inside. I read each year carefully and was in disbelief. None of it made sense to me. I sat for a while and tried to sort it out in my mind. I couldn't grasp what I was reading. I carefully reread each one. Finally, I realized something was very wrong.

I grabbed my purse and keys and locked the doors. I got into the car and drove quickly to see my mother's best friend, Annette. She had also been my parents' accountant.

I rang her doorbell. When she opened the door, I began speaking at a ridiculous rate that no one would have been able to understand. She tried to calm me down. She invited me to come inside. She put her arms around me to try to comfort me.

"Annette, I need for you to explain some things to me that I don't understand."

I was crying and trembling.

"How did my family live such a lavish lifestyle with the sum of money both of my parents made?"

When she looked at me, I knew she felt my pain. I could see the expression on her face. I knew at once that something was very wrong. She became flustered and at a loss for words.

"I need to know the truth! Someone needs to tell me. You know the truth. I know you do. I can't live my life wondering if any of it was real. At this point, my imagination is probably far worse than anything you could tell me."

I begged for answers. Annette could easily see I was distraught. We sat at the kitchen table. She asked me to leave it alone, but I was relentless. I wanted her to tell me the truth. With tears in her eyes, she told me what she knew about my parents.

"Your mother had you when she was seventeen. She was five months pregnant when she married Nickie. There was a shotgun wedding before you were born. Your grandparents were very religious. There had never been anything like it in the family before. Her family disowned her and threw her out of the house. She had nowhere to go. She had no choice but to live with your biological father, Nickie, and his parents."

I sat quietly and listened. I could see Annette was struggling with every word. I knew it was a conversation she had never expected to have with me. It was emotional for both of us.

"Nickie had a gambling problem. He had a

hiotory of passing had checks. He ended up in prison. Your mother divorced Nickie when he was inside. Nickie was a violent man. He got out and went looking for her and beat her up when he found her. Your mother was in the hospital for a few months. After that, she was terrified of him. She went into hiding with you.

"Unfortunately, she had a lot of bad luck along the way. Nickie's parents died in a car accident. They were no longer around to help her financially. The lovely lady you were both living with died in her sleep. Then you got sick. There were medical bills your mother couldn't afford to pay. She didn't even make enough to pay the rent. Her landlord evicted her from her apartment.

"Life was not working out very well for her. She was alone in the world. She had to drop out of high school, so she didn't have a skill that she could use to find a job that would support the both of you. The only job she could find was waiting tables. She couldn't make enough money to pay the bills. She ended up leaving you with people she thought would take care of you and keep you safe. Then she went on to do what she had to do to survive.

"I know this is going to be hard for you to

hear. Gina introduced Josie to a world of darkness: full of seedy characters, narcotics, gambling, and prostitution. Once you entered the life, you could never get out. Josie wasn't strong enough to head off the disastrous chain of events that would follow."

She had confirmed my worst fears. After many hours of hearing the truth, I left. I got into the car and cried all the way to Tim's house. Tim was my stepfather Jason's nephew. He and my mother had had a special friendship. I showed up on his doorstep and pleaded with Tim as I had with Annette. I was convincing.

"Daniella, I am begging you. You need to leave this alone. Your parents are dead. Let them rest in peace. Your mother never did anything your father didn't know about."

He looked at me with grave concern.

"I will tell you, that is why Jason's family didn't like your mother. They didn't like the lifestyle your parents were living. Of course, they blamed everything on your mom."

"Why didn't she stop when they got married?"

I impatiently awaited his response.

"I don't believe Jason's work was consistent enough to pay the bills. They struggled financially through the years. It was the one thing they had that could get them through the difficult times."

"Why did we move from our charming two-bedroom house? I woke up one morning, and there was a 'For Sale' sign in the front yard. It has always bothered me."

"Jason found out your mother had been set up one night with one of the neighbors. By morning, everyone in the neighborhood knew. It embarrassed and upset Jason. That was why they got into the fight. It was also the reason you moved."

"I always knew there was more to that story."

"Leave it alone, Daniella! I have said enough already. There is nothing more that you need to know."

We drank coffee and then I went home. That night, I recalled a conversation I'd had with my stepfather, Jason. He had told me my mom struggled with some things she had done in her life. She was suffering from anxiety. He asked me to try to be understanding of her mood swings. There were times when she refused to leave the house alone.

Jason took her to a psychiatrist. I didn't understand then, but it all made sense to me now. I had a pit in my stomach. I wanted the truth, and now I had it. I figured out where my mother got the new Cadillacs, mink coats, expensive clothes, and jewelry. I now knew how we had lived such a beautiful lifestyle.

I chuckled to myself. There had been times when the kids at school bullied me. I never understood why. It turns out that they were jealous. I had the best of everything and some of them didn't. I wonder what they would think now if they knew how we had managed to live the way we did. I wondered if any of my classmates knew anything about my parents. It horrified me to think that some of them or all of them may have known.

I finally found out why we went to Miami. Gina had a connection to Big Al and the boys. Big Al had a connection to the hotel in North Florida. Together, they set my mother up. I could no longer deny the fact that my mother had been a call girl.

My stepfather, Jason, knew. He accepted my mother's lifestyle. Jason spent the money like the rest of us. On that day, he fell from the pedestal I had placed him on so long ago. It was impossible for me to understand how he could allow my mother to be with other men. It made me sick to my stomach. How could I ever forgive him? I couldn't believe this was the man that I knew and loved. I had been so proud to call him my father.

My mother had told me long ago to leave it alone. I wished I had, but I didn't listen. I wondered how I would get past the knowledge I had gained. Just when I thought my life hadn't been confusing enough, it got even worse. I was heartbroken, but I finally had closure. Knowing the truth was not as easy as I thought it would be. I concluded that sometimes not knowing is better, but it was too late. I had gone searching for the truth, and I had found it. Now I could spend the rest of my life trying to figure out how to live with it.

# Chapter

## Twenty-six

*Y*ears went by, and I finally processed the events of the year my mother died. I thought of all the pain and suffering my mother had endured. It must have been terrible for her. Her life would have turned out differently if abortion had been legal. My mom wouldn't have lost her family and she could have had a normal life. She wouldn't have had to care for us on her own. On the other hand, if abortion had been legal, I wouldn't be here today. I am truly grateful for the sacrifices my mother made to give me life. I am happy I have had the chance to live. I have loved and felt loved. I have had my share of heartbreak and suffering, but even after everything I have been through, I would have wanted to live. No one ever said life was going to be easy.

I lay in bed one night and said a prayer. I made a promise to myself, God, and my mother that I would live every day as if it were my last. I told her I could not let the pain and suffering that she had endured to give me life be for nothing. I thanked my mother for all she had given up letting me live.

I thanked my stepfather, Jason, for loving me as much as any father could. He had shown his love for me every day. Without him, I don't know where I would be today. He made me believe that if I put my mind to it, I could do anything. He gave me strength and courage. His faith in me helped me to build a better life for myself.

I struggled with the knowledge I had gained in my quest for the truth. In the end, I realized the only thing that mattered was the unconditional love Jason had given to me. The only right answer seemed to be to give him the same unconditional love in return. It's been twenty years since he passed. I still think about him every day.

I could never forgive Nickie, but I finally

understood why he didn't want anything to do with me. Sadly, he was the only person who had been honest with me. Had I not gone looking for the truth, I wouldn't have had to live with the fallout from our encounter. It's a sharp reminder every day that there are always at least two sides to every story.

I wrote this book with love and affection for those families who took care of me when my mother couldn't.

Gina, wherever you are, I will always have a special place in my heart for you.

My bond with Big Al and the boys will live on forever.

My mother was a fighter, and so was I. We fought different battles and with a different style, but we each learned how to take care of ourselves.

I didn't have a home or a family. I was alone and afraid. I wanted someone to take care of me. Then one day, I realized I was making bad choices. I couldn't take any more disappointment or heartbreak. I refused to continue to believe someone else was going to take care of me. I knew I needed to do a better job of taking care of myself. I was certain the only way I could was to become financially independent.

I was a woman starting a career with limited resources. I had a high school education and no business skills. I wasn't qualified to make much more than minimum wage. I worked during the day and went to a university at night. I took one class a semester. My company offered free computer training at a computer school. I took more than a hundred hours of classes. They paid for me to take other courses to help me advance in my job. I enthusiastically enrolled in all of them. It took years of night school, but I finally finished junior college.

I didn't have a personal life. I didn't want anything to interfere with my performance at work. I was fighting for survival. My goal was to climb the corporate ladder. I knew I would have to start at the bottom and work my way up. I had to work exceptionally hard to prove myself. It took years for anyone to take me seriously.

My employer finally recognized me for my efforts. I got every promotion I set my sights on. I started to make enough money to take care of myself. I got a real estate license and a Community Association Manager's license. Then one day it happened. I became financially independent. I stopped being afraid. I had built a nice life for myself, all by myself. I didn't have parents, and I didn't have siblings. All I had was me. One day, I sat back and marveled at all I had achieved despite my rocky beginnings. I owned my home, and I had created my own personal space. I no longer needed someone to take care of me. I could afford to take care of myself.

That's when I realized that I was worthy of being happy. I gradually started to change the image I had of myself. I was slowly becoming more confident. Once I did, the quality of my life began to improve. I was comfortable being more selective in my relationship choices. I was no longer willing to allow "takers" into my world. I began filling my life with more loving, kind, and sincere people. I was no longer making decisions out of need or fear.

Today I have a career and a lovely little house. I emotionally adopted a beautiful young girl who appreciates motherly love. She has been my friend and my rock for the last seventeen years. She is everything I would ever have wanted a biological daughter to be. I feel blessed to have her in my life. I have wonderful friends and a cute little dog. I have had a terrific man in my life now for nearly five years. It is all I have ever needed or wanted.

It isn't always easy to find happiness, but it's

never too late. It took a lot of hard work and perseverance, but I am proof it can happen.

I will never understand where I found the strength to sift through the rubble and create a meaningful and productive life for myself. I wish it hadn't been so hard, but I think the experiences in my life made me a better person. It took years, but I finally found peace. We can't change our pasts; we can only grow from them and use the knowledge we gain to create a better future.

I no longer look in the mirror and feel sadness. I am proud of my accomplishments. I no longer feel ashamed of my past. I am comfortable with the person I have become. It is that comfort that has given me the courage to share my story.

# About the Author

This book is the story of my life. In the beginning, putting the words on paper was my therapy. In the end, I wanted to share my story with the hope that it would inspire those who read it.

What I have learned in my quest for happiness:

- We all deserve to be happy.
- Life isn't fair.
- We are not always in control of what happens.
- Don't ever let anyone mistreat you. If you let them, they will continue. That's your fault, not theirs.
- Don't waste time on *why*s or *what-if*s.
- Don't rely on others to make you happy.
- You can't change your past.
- You can create a better future.
- Most importantly, never give up!

Life is short and precious. *Take responsibility for creating your own happiness.* Then you own it! Don't ever let anyone take it away from you!

# Acknowledgments

Harlan: During every step of this journey, I remembered what you said: "You're finishing the book." Thank you, love! I finished the book! Without you, I don't know if I would have ever done it.

Jenniffer: Thank you for always being there for me and for your continued encouragement.

The Snyder family: My book has taken years to finish. Writing it made me revisit many painful events in my life. Without the support of some of the most wonderful people I have ever known, I am not certain I would have had the courage to get through it.

Tina and Arnie: Thank you for your critique of my manuscript and your love, guidance, and support. I will always be grateful.

Barbara and Warren: Thank you for reading my manuscript. Your input meant a lot to me.

Jayne: I made many corrections based on your great notes.

Robert: Thank you for your guidance and support.

There have been too many wonderful and supportive people in my life to mention them all. You know who you are, and I feel blessed to have you in my life.